Adobe Premiere Pro Power Tips

Adobe Premiere Pro Power Tips

SECRETS, SHORTCUTS, AND TECHNIQUES

By Larry Jordan

Focal Press
Taylor & Francis Group

NEW YORK AND LONDON

First published 2013
by Focal Press
70 Blanchard Road, Suite 402, Burlington, MA 01803

Simultaneously published in the UK
by Focal Press
2 Park Square, Milton Park, Abingdon, Oxon OX14 4RN

Focal Press is an imprint of the Taylor & Francis Group, an informa business

Library of Congress Cataloging in Publication Data
Jordan, Larry, 1950-
  Adobe Premiere pro power tips / by Larry Jordan.
     pages cm
  Includes bibliographical references.
1. Motion pictures—Editing—Data processing. 2. Digital video—Editing—Data processing.
3. Adobe Premiere. I. Title.
  TR899.J6698 2014
  777'.55—dc23
                                    2012031762

ISBN: 978-0-415-65707-5 (pbk)
ISBN: 978-0-203-06754-3 (ebk)

Typeset in ITC Legacy Serif Std
Project Managed and Typeset by: diacriTech

Printed in the United States of America by Courier, Kendallville, Indiana

Dedication

To an incredible team: Tori Anderholt,
Cirina Catania, Laura Peters,
Debbie Price, Patrick Saxon, and
Mina Qubaisi.

Contents

Welcome

This is my favorite kind of book—because it is filled with hidden tips, keyboard shortcuts, and little-known productivity boosters. This is the good stuff that takes you under the hood and shows you how to *really* get your work done faster.

As both an editor and a businessman, I've discovered that there is never enough time to get everything done that I need to do. If I can learn a skill or shortcut or technique that can save me a few seconds for something I do frequently, that means a lot. Video editing, even with the best software, takes a long time. And time is a precious commodity.

Adobe Production Premium has millions of devoted users around the world, with lots of books that show how to run the software. I don't need to repeat their work. Instead, this book picks up where those books end—this book shows you how to run this software *better*.

Plus, with the release of the brand new CS6 edition, we've included hundreds of tips specifically designed to get you up to speed on this new software fast! (We actually lost count of how many tips are in this book, but it approaches a thousand ...)

If you enjoy figuring things out on your own, don't buy this book.

But if you are more interested in getting your work done on time, on budget, and with great quality—this book is for you. Best of all, you don't need to read it cover to cover; just jump in anywhere. Each chapter looks at one aspect of the software. Each tip is designed to take a page or less.

Discover just how cool being really productive can be!

What This Book Covers

This book covers Adobe Story, Prelude, Premiere Pro, Audition, and Media Encoder. Each program has its own chapter, except for Premiere, which has several chapters devoted to it. Although there are far more packages in the Adobe Production Premium than just those five, this book doesn't have room to cover everything.

Each tip contains a title, subtitle, screen shot (in most cases), and the tip, plus lots and lots of notes and personal recommendations.

My biggest concern with writing any book is that I miss something obvious or forget to include your favorite shortcut. If you have a technique that you think should be in this book, send me an e-mail at Larry@LarryJordan.biz and I'll add it to the collection for the next edition of this book.

How This Book Is Organized

This book is organized around the production process. It starts with planning, then flows through scripting, shooting, logging, editing, audio mixing and final output. Premiere Pro may be the center of our editing world, but there are a lot of other activities and applications that revolve around it.

Chapter 1 covers planning and getting our systems ready for editing. Chapter 2 provides tips on using Adobe Story for script-writing and production planning. Chapter 3 showcases how to use the brand-new Prelude to review, log and capture tapeless media. Chapters 4–7, and 9 explore hundreds of hidden features in Premiere Pro. Chapter 8 takes us on a side trip to one of my favorite programs—Audition—which can really make audio sound great. Then, we wrap up with Chapter 10, covering output, export, and compression using Adobe Media Encoder.

I am a huge fan of workflow, of avoiding wasting time and energy and concentrating on doing the right task the right way at the right time. You don't need to read these chapters in order—though reading Chapter 1 first will answer a lot of basic questions—but I wanted to share with you the thinking that went into organizing all the tips in this book.

Thanks for the Images

One of the hardest things in writing a book is licensing images. (I've discovered it often takes longer to license footage than to write the book.)

To that end, I'd like to thank:

- Dr. Vint Cerf and Alcatel/Lucent for the interview with Dr. Vint Cert. This was conducted in 2004, during Dr. Cerf's visit to Van Nuys High School, California, where he was encouraging students to stay in school and study math and science.

- Pond5 (www.pond5.com) for a selection of clips from their outstanding collection of royalty-free media.

- John Putch, producer/director of the dramatic film *Route 30, Too!* (www.route30trilogy.com).

- Fran and Miles Hale of Model Railroad Builders (www.modelrailroadbuilders.com) for their outstanding model railroad scenery footage.

- Michael Shaw for the shaky camera and rolling shutter footage.

- NASA for their outer space videos.

- Smartsound for music and sound effects files (www.smartsound.com).

All screen shots are taken from the CS6 release of the software.

Check Out Our Website

We've put together a companion website with video tutorials that amplify many of the tips offered in this book.

Visit www.focalpress.com/9780415657075 to see these tips in action.

Special People to Thank

Heading the list of people to thank is Tim Kolb, Adobe Certified Master Trainer, who rashly volunteered to tech edit this book. The fact that these tips make any sense at all is due to Tim's eternal vigilance … and long e-mail conversations. Visit his website at www.kolbproductions.com. It was a delight working with him.

Tori Anderholt is next on my list. An outstanding researcher and organizer of the unorganizable, she was invaluable in finding, collecting, and managing all of those loose slips of paper filled with "great ideas." This book would not exist without Tori's help.

I also want to thank the folks at Adobe Systems, Inc.: Michelle Galina, Kevin Monahan, and the entire Production Premium team who took time to look over early chapters, provide voluminous comments, and, in general, tried to keep me from running off the rails.

The people at Focal Press also deserve mention: Dennis McGonagle, an acquisition editor who refused to take no at face value, and Lauren Mattos and her entire production team for turning this book into something beautiful.

Finally, I owe a deep debt to my team here at Larry Jordan & Associates Inc., who have learned to dread the words "I've decided to write another book." I could not do what I do without their incredible help and I count on them more than I can possibly express.

Still, in spite of the support of these great people, this book is my responsibility. If there are errors, I apologize and will correct them in the next revision.

Last Thought

If I have to be honest, I have to admit that I really don't like writing a book. I've created hundreds of hours of online training and tens of thousands of pages of technical articles, step-by-step guides, product reviews, and all the other elements that populate my website (www.larryjordan.biz).

But a book is different. In my mind it needs to be better, more accurate, more complete, and more precise than anything that I write for the web. And that sets a high bar to meet.

I am writing these final words after the rest of the book is complete. I just finished editing the final draft before sending it to the publisher. In looking over the entire manuscript, I am really proud of this book.

There are tips here that will save you hours of editing. There's an "ah-HA!" moment lurking on almost every page. And I've added tons of explanations that not only show you what to do but *why* you should do it.

In this technology-driven, budget-challenged, rapidly changing world, it is sometimes hard to remember why we got into this bizarre business. We are storytellers—and don't let the tools you use distract you from that core fact. Everything we do is designed to captivate the mind, heart, and soul of an audience. That's what makes all the hard work so much fun!

I may not like writing, but I love having written. Enjoy—you're gonna have a great time with this book!

Larry Jordan
Los Angeles
July 2012

CHAPTER 1

Get Ready

Welcome!

The goal of this book is to help you become faster and more proficient. But before we start editing, we need to get ready. This chapter covers the basics—from showing how to organize your system to explaining scratch disks and video formats. Much of the material that we cover here applies to all of the media applications in Production Premium.

Let's start by getting organized.

Use a Project Code to Track Your Projects

I, uh, stole this system from Hollywood

Several years ago, I was editing behind-the-scenes documentaries for inclusion on DVDs created by two of the major Hollywood studios and I noticed that all of their master tapes had a consistent project number:

- A two-letter code for the show

- A single number for the season of the show

- A two-number code for the episode of the show within that season

(Continued)

Hmmm ... this was such an efficient way to track projects that I borrowed the idea. Because I don't do network series work but do do a lot of corporate work, I dropped the series number and created my own Project Code:

- Two letters that represent the name of the client
- Two numbers that represent the particular job for a client

For example, in the illustration given here, "JM" refers to the client—"Just a Moment Productions"—and the numbers refer to the third job we did for this client.

A Folder-Naming System for Tapeless Media

Get organized from the very beginning

The most important rule to keep in mind when working with tapeless media is that you are handling the master footage from the camera. **Back It Up!** Most professional editors who are working with tapeless media make at least three copies of the card. Storage is cheap compared to reshooting a scene.

Second, always copy the entire contents of the card to its own folder on your hard disk. Never copy just a portion of the card.

Also, I strongly recommend not storing media to the boot disk; rather, use a second drive. (The "boot disk" is the hard drive that contains your Applications folder and operating system.) For instance, on that second drive, I create a folder called **Source Media**, which will contain the source media for each project.

Each of these folders follows a consistent folder structure:

- Within the **Source Media** folder, I create a folder for each client or series. (Blue)
- Within the **Client** folder, I create a folder for each project. (Orange)

(Continued)

- Within the **Project** folder, I create a folder for each card, and give each folder a consistent name. (Yellow) I always store the *entire* contents of each camera card in its own folder.

For example, in the screen shot given here, my folder name starts with the Project Code, followed by the date the card was shot, followed by a reference for whether this is the A/B/C camera, followed by the card number for that camera (first card shot, second card shot, third card shot, and so on).

Now I can tell at a glance, simply by looking at the folder name, who the client was, what the job number was, the date it was shot, and which camera was used.

Prelude and Premiere Pro both track this folder name during ingest so that if at any point in the future, you need to go back and recapture footage, both of these programs know exactly where it is.

Keep in mind that it is a lot easier—and faster—to get organized at the beginning of a project than at the end when both deadlines and tempers are short.

Which Files Should Be Copied From a Camera Card?

Everyone is in a hurry; what's the minimum number of files that need to be copied?

All of them. Absolutely everything on the card needs to be copied. No exceptions.

Select the entire contents of the card, even the folders and files that you don't recognize, and copy the entire contents of the card into its own folder on your hard disk.

Always.

Is There a Better Way to Copy Files Than Using the Operating System?

Prelude should be your first choice for copying files

Adobe Prelude CS6 is designed to easily copy tapeless media files from the camera card to your hard disk.

If, for some reason, Prelude isn't available, there is a great utility for both Mac and Windows that simplifies the file copy process called: Shotput Pro, by Imagine Products (www.imagineproducts.com). Other options include media handling utilities from most of the camera manufacturers.

Shotput Pro, like Prelude, allows you to copy files to multiple destinations, verifies the accuracy of file copies, and works at a very high speed.

Why Not Store Media on the Boot Disk?

You can, but it isn't a wise decision

The basic problem with storing media on your boot disk, or boot drive (I use the terms interchangeably) is that the boot drive is too distracted to pay proper attention.

The absolute top priority for the boot drive is finding and recording data for the operating system. The second priority is processing data for the active foreground application. The third priority is handling data for background applications.

Then, there's media, with a priority down near dirt. Yet what do we need to play consistently, second after second, megabyte after megabyte? Right—media. Well, those poor hard disks are going nuts trying to meet all these conflicting needs quickly; so playing media gets shuffled off to "play media whenever possible."

(Continued)

It is far better to move your media to a second drive reserved just for data. You'll be surprised at just how much more efficient your system becomes.

Are USB Drives Fast Enough for Video Editing?

It depends upon your operating system

USB 2.0 drives are only recommended for archiving, not media playback; they are too slow. While they can play some versions of limited-file-size video, this is really not a good idea.

USB 3.0 drives on a PC are generally fast enough to support many video formats. This format is just now starting to show up on Macintosh computers, so the jury is still out on how fast these drives will be; however, while USB 2 is not fast enough on Macintosh system, USB 3 should be OK.

What if I Have, or Want to Add, an SSD Drive?

Ssd drive performance continues to improve

Over the last year or two, the performance of SSD (Solid-State Device) drives has truly improved. In many cases, SSD drives are faster than traditional hard disks. They can speed operations, but they may not be the best choice for media.

While it could be argued that boot drives that use SSD technology are fast enough to also support media playback, I would still advise against it, for the following reasons:

- SSD drives are limited in the amount of storage they support.
- SSD drives are still more expensive than traditional hard disks for the same amount of storage.
- When compared to traditional hard disks, SSD drives have limited reads and writes.

(Continued)

5

Based on talking with technical experts, I recommend using an SSD drive as either your boot drive, or to store cache files. Most of the CS6 applications load files into memory as the application launches. By storing these cache files on an SSD drive, you are able to maximize the performance of your system by putting the files the application needs most frequently on the fastest hard drive.

If your system supports multiple SSD drives, dedicating one SSD for the cache and a second SSD drive for the boot disk provides a significant performance boost.

However, due to the limited storage space and cost of SSD drives, I recommend using standard hard drives for media playback.

It Isn't Just the Size, It's the Speed

Always use at least two hard drives for video editing

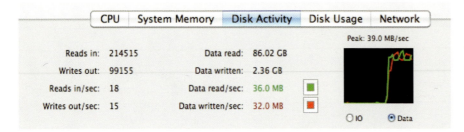

Video editing devours storage. It seems like a hard drive has one of two states: empty or full. So we obsess about how much storage we have, or need, or may potentially-at-some-point-in-the-future need.

But this focuses on the wrong issue. The amount of storage we have is important, but how fast we can transfer data from hard disk to computer and back is far more important. The speed of moving data is called the data transfer rate.

Always use at least two hard drives—whether internal or external—for video editing. Store the application on your boot drive and all media and projects on your second drive.

An easy way to measure hard disk speed on the Macintosh is using **Utilities > Activity Monitor**. Select **Window > Activity Monitor** to display the main

(*Continued*)

window. Click the **Disk Activity** tab during any hard disk operation and watch the green and red numbers. *Data read/sec* indicates the speed of data playback from your hard disk to your computer. *Data written/sec* indicates the speed of data transferred from your computer to your hard disk. The chart to the right provides a visual display of the data transfer over time.

Windows users can use speed utilities provided by AJA, BlackMagic Design, and ATTO, or a universal benchmark utility like HD Speed.

You can run both Activity Monitor and any other application, such as Premiere, at the same time so that you can see what's happening while you are editing. I do this all the time: first, because I like watching the chart; and, second, because it allows me to monitor my storage performance in real time.

Connections Are Everything

How you connect your hard drive determines the speed

Connecting a hard drive via USB 3 is a very fast way to connect a drive, provided you are on a PC. However, until recently, USB 3 was not supported on the Mac. So Mac users should connect their hard drives using FireWire 800; FireWire 400 is about one-third the speed of FireWire 800.

An even better solution is Thunderbolt. This new format from Intel and Apple provides data transfer rates up to twenty times faster than either USB or FireWire. The only problem is that Thunderbolt is so new that there are not a lot of storage systems that support it at the time of writing. This should change quickly in the coming months.

Thunderbolt

Thunderbolt can be especially helpful as you start working with multicam projects, where you are editing multiple camera angles at the same time.

Note: Thunderbolt has roughly the same bandwidth as a single PCIe slot.

Picking the Right Storage

Size alone is not enough

When it comes to storage, total capacity is important, but not the most important. Here are other factors to consider:

- How it's connected. Thunderbolt, FireWire 800, USB 3, and eSATA are all good options. Gigabit Ethernet or iSCSI can work for some formats, but this is not good enough for multicamera editing.

- Rotation speed. Although not as important as in the past, with all other things being equal, faster rotation speed is better. However, you won't notice any significant difference in a single drive that turns at 10,000 rpm versus a drive that spins at 7200 rpm. How the drive is connected to the computer will limit any speed improvements caused by faster rotational speed.

- Internal versus external. Internal single drives are generally faster than external single drives. However, replacing or upgrading an external drive is easier than replacing an internal drive.

- SSD drives are likely to be faster than spinning hard drives—provided that you have a newer computer running the SSD drive—but SSD drives are much more expensive and they don't hold as much data. Generally, use SSD drives to store cache files and standard spinning hard drives for media.

- A RAID (Redundant Array of Independent Disks) is better than a single drive, but it costs more. RAIDs are faster, hold more and, provided they are RAID 5 or 6, protect your data in the event of a drive failure within the unit.

Pick the Right RAID

Different RAID types have different purposes

RAIDs are categorized by type or level. Once you understand what these types mean, you can pick the best RAID for your needs.

Data protection means your data is safe if a drive in the RAID fails. RAID speed is determined both by the RAID and how the RAID is connected to your computer. Even the fastest RAID can be significantly slowed by a slow connection to the computer.

The Minimum Drives column in this table specifies the minimum number of drives needed for that configuration. Most RAIDs, except for Type 0 and 1, ship with many more drives than the minimum.

Raid Type	Min. Drives	Benefit	Limitation
0	2	Fast, inexpensive	No redundancy. If you lose one drive, you lose all your data
1	2	Inexpensive, data protection	Slow, equals the speed and storage of a single hard drive
5	3	Very fast, data protection	More expensive, protects against failure of a single drive
6	4	Very fast, data protection	Slightly more expensive, protects against failure of two drives
50	6	Wicked fast, data protection	It ain't cheap.
60	8	Really wicked fast, data protection	It *really* ain't cheap.

For a RAID to take on the road, I prefer RAID 0—small, fast, and cheap.

For capturing tapeless media on set, when you absolutely, positively MUST capture and protect everything, I prefer RAID 1. RAID 1 essentially duplicates

(Continued)

your date to two hard drives simultaneously in real time. Although you can use a pair of separate hard disks, a RAID 1 does the same thing in a single package.

For normal editing, I prefer RAID 5.

For high-speed support of a group of editors, I prefer RAID 50.

How Much and How Fast

This table shows speeds and sizes of common video formats

Trying to decide how much storage space you need for your next project? Wondering how fast your hard disks need to be? This table can help. It lists common video formats on the left, the speed of data transfer in the middle, and the space necessary to store one hour of media on the right. (Data transfer is the speed media files need to move between your storage and the computer.)

Video Format	Data Transfer Rate	Space to Store 1 Hour for 1 Hour of Media
DV (NTSC or PAL)	3.75 MB/second	13 GB
JVC HDV (NTSC or PAL)	2.5 MB/second	8.9 GB
Canon / Sony HDV	3.75 MB/sec	13 GB
AVCHD	1.5 – 3 MB/sec	10.5 GB
Canon DSLR	4.75 MB/sec	17.1 GB
XDCAM EX	4.4 MB/sec	15.8 GB
XDCAM HD422	6.25 MB/sec	22.5 GB
AVC-Intra	12.5 MB/sec	45 GB
ProRes 422	18.1 MB/sec	65 GB
R3D (native)	38 MB/sec	133 GB

*Note: File sizes and transfer rates for HD media often vary depending on image size and frame rate. These numbers are for 720p/60 HD media, except for R3D files.

What's A Scratch Disk?

Scratch disks are where media goes to live

Whether you are working with audio, video, or images, editing media requires lots of different files. Some files are created by you, others by the application. These work files need to be stored somewhere. So, by tradition, the "Scratch Disk" is what we call the drive location where these work files are stored.

Generally, there are multiple files and folders associated with each project that are stored on the scratch disk. For example, in addition to traditional media files, work files could also include volume data and waveform displays used by Audition, metadata files created by Prelude, or render files created by Premiere Pro.

These all need a home, on your "scratch disk."

Configure Your Media Drives

Use multiple hard drives for best performance

When you install Adobe's video applications, they create a whole lot of additional folders for media, temporary working files, templates, and others. These work files are stored on "Scratch Disks," which Adobe also calls "Media Drives."

These files are created by the software to store media, facilitate performance, simplify editing, preview files, and so on. Some files are permanent, while other files are needed frequently and quickly but are often wasteful to archive, and they can be recreated if lost with no additional data.

Earlier, I mentioned storing these files on a second drive. That process is called "setting" or "pointing" your media drives.

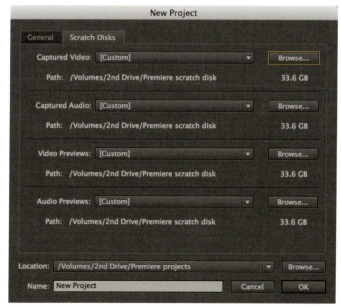

(Continued)

Depending on your system, this second drive could be either an internal drive or an external drive. However, it must not be a partition of your boot drive. Partitioning simply takes your existing drive and subdivides it. Partitions are *not* faster than an unpartitioned drive.

For my editing, I have one folder on my second drive that holds project files and a second folder on my second drive that holds media files. You can, if you want, use a different organization system for your projects. The key is to be sure they are never stored on your boot drive.

Where Are Media Files Stored by Default?

Default locations are not optimal—or even recommended

For software developers, the only hard disk location on your Mac that a developer knows will definitely exist is your Home directory. (Windows uses a similar user-based location, but it isn't called the "Home directory.") They know that specific location exists, that it belongs specifically to you, and they know exactly how to find it.

So, that means that, by default, any time a developer needs to store something somewhere—such as preferences, templates, media, work files—they will store it somewhere within this Home directory. However, this is not an ideal location for large files, files that need to be shared between editors, or files that need to playback without interruption.

In later chapters, I'll show you which preferences to adjust to optimize your system for best performance by moving the location of these media files.

What Files Can You Safely Keep in Your Home Directory?

Not all files need to move

Many of the files that Adobe stores in your Home directory can stay there. The general rule is: "If the file doesn't need to play back in real time, or doesn't need to be shared with others, you can leave it in your Home directory."

So preference files are perfectly fine remaining where Adobe put them.

However, as mentioned earlier, media files should be moved to a second drive. Also, if you want to share template files with other editors, they should be moved either to shared storage (i.e., a server) or an external drive.

Files that don't play in real time—for example, Photoshop documents or text files—can be stored anywhere. I generally store them with project files, but this is for organizational, not technical, reasons.

Can Multiple Editors Work on the Same Project?

Other than from story, CS6 projects are not multiuser

The short answer is "no," multiple editors can't work on the same project. But there's a lot of wiggle room in that statement. Also, the newly-announced Adobe Anywhere, which is scheduled for release in 2013, completely changes this answer because it is specifically designed for multiple editors to work on the same project.

Story was built from the ground up to allow multiple people to collaborate on the same project—from scripts to production schedules, people can write, correct, review, and read the same materials. This speeds up the whole preproduction planning and communication process.

Prelude is designed as a single-user application; however, the benefit to using Prelude for logging and capturing media is that an editorial assistant

(Continued)

13

can be logging clips while an editor is busy in Premiere editing clips that Prelude has captured. Although only one person is using each application, or writing to the project files, multiple people can contribute elements to the same project.

Also, with Premiere Pro, although only one person can be saving files, if you have the right software, for example, Edit Share (www.editshare.com/), more than one person can view a Premiere project, although only one person can save changes to it. This allows multiple editors to, say, copy clips from a common project containing opens and bumpers, while each editor is working and saving their individual specific project.

What Is the Mercury Playback Engine?

It's hardware, or software, that speeds effects

"Mercury Playback Engine" is a name for a large number of performance improvements in Adobe Premiere Pro CS5 and later. It is based on either hardware or software. If you have a supported graphics card (GPU), this acceleration is handled by the card. If you don't, this acceleration is handled in the software. (Acceleration via hardware is always faster.)

Premiere automatically uses whichever acceleration technology is available. This acceleration yields faster real-time effects, image scaling, less rendering, and greater time-savings. The benefits of the Mercury Playback engine include:

- Support for more CPU processors via multithreading

- Processing of some tasks using CUDA (and OpenCL in Premiere Pro CS6)

CUDA is an NVidia technology (architecture, programming language, etc.) for a certain kind of GPU processing. Because CUDA is from NVidia, only NVidia cards provide it. OpenCL is a technology that is similar in purpose to CUDA. OpenCL features are provided by many graphics cards, including ATI/AMD cards.

(Continued)

Visit www.adobe.com/products/premiere/tech-specs.html for the official and up-to-date list of the cards that provide the CUDA/OpenCL processing features. Not all cards are supported.

On Macintosh systems, support for OpenCL processing for the Mercury Playback Engine requires recent MacBook Pro laptops and Mac OS X v10.7.x or later.

What Does the Mercury Playback Engine Do?

It speeds many effects and rendering, but it doesn't work miracles

The Mercury Playback Engine improves the speed of:

- Rendering for preview and final output
- More than forty visual effects
- Image scaling
- Deinterlacing
- Blending modes
- Color space conversions

It does not affect the speed of encoding or decoding media. Also, the Mercury Playback Engine only supports Premiere Pro CS5 or later.

In CS6, the Mercury Playback Engine Powers Some MacBook Pros

Hardware acceleration now available in hardware mode using open CL

There are two flavors of the Mercury Playback Engine—a fast version that runs using software and

(Continued)

15

a screaming fast version that uses the hardware graphics card that you have in your system.

In the past, only computers with certain NVIDIA cards could take advantage of Premiere's hardware acceleration, which left out almost all Macs. Now, with the CS6 release, specific recent MacBook Pro computers running the ATI Radeon HD 6750M or 6770M graphics card are accelerated as well.

There's nothing you need to turn on. As Premiere starts up, it checks to see what card you have on your system. If it finds a match, Premiere turns on hardware acceleration. If it doesn't, it turns on software acceleration. Either way, things start moving very quickly after that.

You can see which version of the Mercury Playback Engine your system is using by selecting **Project > Project Settings > General**.

You need to be running OS X 10.7 (Lion), or later, to take advantage of hardware acceleration on a MacBook Pro.

What Is Field Dominance?

Don't let field dominance intimidate you

There are two ways to shoot video:

- Progressive, which shoots all the lines of the frame at one time.

- Interlaced, which shoots every other line of video then, a split second later, shoots the remaining lines. For instance, first all of the odd-numbered lines are shot, then the even-numbered lines.

We grew up with interlaced video. Both NTSC and PAL use it, as do some HD formats. Progressive, however, is the preferred format for computers and the web. (For example, DSLR cameras shoot a progressive image.)

16

(Continued)

Because interlaced footage requires shooting one set of lines a fraction of a second before the other, it is important to know when set of lines was shot first—otherwise, your image won't play back properly.

- Upper field dominant means that all of the odd-numbered lines were shot first.

- Lower field dominant means that all of the even-numbered lines were shot first.

All standard-definition formats (NTSC and PAL) shoot interlaced video, except when shooting 24 fps, which is progressive.

HD formats are interlaced if they describe the video format as 1080i. The letter "i" indicates an interlaced format. HD formats are progressive if they describe the video format at 1080p. The letter "p" indicates a progressive format.

All 720p formats are progressive. (I know, it's enough to drive you nuts!)

2K and 4K formats shoot progressive images.

If you are shooting interlaced NTSC or PAL DV standard-definition video, set Field Dominance to Lower when creating a new Sequence; both of these formats shoot all the even lines in your image first. (I'll explain how to set interlacing later, in Chapter 4.)

If you are shooting PAL or NTSC broadcast formats, such as DigiBetacam or Betacam SP, set Field Dominance to Upper, as both of these formats shoot all the odd lines first.

If you are shooting interlaced high-definition (HD) video, set Field Dominance to Upper. HD shoots all the odd lines first. Interlaced HD formats use the letter i after the number (e.g., 1080i) to indicate the scanning format.

If you are shooting progressive video, set Field Dominance to None.

Sigh ... such a mess!

Why All This Confusion Over Formats?

Because even the pros can't define the "best" format

There is a *wide* range of incompatible video formats. Different image sizes, different frame rates, different scanning, different compression ... it's enough to drive everyone mad.

Some formats work really well for color grading or effects; others work really well retaining image detail during action. Some have small file sizes, while still others are best suited for final distribution.

Even broadcasters can't agree. For a variety of technical reasons, some of the broadcast networks (CBS, NBC, PBS) standardized on 1080i as their distribution format. Others (ABC, ESPN, FOX) picked 720p.

When planning a new project, it is generally a good idea to figure out what your final delivery requirements are before deciding what format to shoot. In other words, figure out what you need to deliver, then work backward from that.

What Video Format Should I Shoot?

Not all video formats provide the same results

If you don't know your deliverable format, I would recommend shooting 1080p.

Given the choice, shoot progressive video. You can easily convert progressive video to any format. Converting interlaced video to progressive is difficult and generally yields lower quality than shooting progressive.

Although I don't particularly like the compression in AVCHD or H.264, it is a common video format in inexpensive cameras. Another popular, but very

18

(Continued)

compressed, format is XDCAM (and its variants). Because Premiere Pro CS6 can easily edit these formats, they are fine for many projects.

However, for projects designed for theatrical projection, green-screen compositing, or sophisticated color correction and grading, using a camera that shoots RED, AVC-Intra, or ProRes files will yield better image quality, faster render times, and higher-quality output.

When Does Transcoding Make Sense?

Transcoding converts video from one format to another

The Mercury Playback Engine is an amazing piece of work. However, the hardware-accelerated version does not run on all systems. And some video formats are much harder to edit than others. These would include H.264, MPEG-4, and AVCHD.

If you are on a slower system, transcoding, or converting, your media from the format the camera shot (called native) into a format that is easier to edit can save you a lot of time.

Transcoding is also helpful when you have lots of different video formats, frame rates, or image sizes to work with. Transcoding them all into a single standard will make your life a lot easier over the course of a large project.

The Adobe Media Encoder is a good tool for this conversion. Although Adobe does not have a high-end video codec of its own, it does a great job of converting DSLR footage, for example, from H-264 to ProRes, DNxHD, or Cineform. Any of those three formats are good, solid choices that provide high-performance editing while maintaining excellent image quality.

When Should I Delete Files?

Delete unused media to regain storage space

If your Project panel is full to bursting and you want to get rid of files that you are not using, there's a very simple way to do this. Best of all, this just removes them from the Project panel; it does NOT delete any media on your hard drive.

To do this:

1. Save your project to capture its current state. (This allows you to bring everything back, just in case you delete the wrong file, by selecting **File > Revert**.)

2. Choose **Project > Remove Unused**. This removes all unused files from the Project panel.

3. Examine your project. If it looks okay, save your project. Otherwise, choose **Edit > Undo** to restore the files that you removed.

This does *not* affect any clips edited in your sequences, nor does it remove any files from your hard disk.

Premiere Fully Supports RED

But you may want to tweak the source settings

Some camera formats, and RED comes first to mind, provide additional controls over their video settings using the Source Settings panel.

To access these controls, right-click the name of a clip in the Project panel or Viewer. If Source Settings is not grayed out, your video format provides additional controls. For instance, the RED Source Controls window gives you full control over RED parameters and allows R3D files to be imported, both as QuickTime proxies and RAW files.

(Continued)

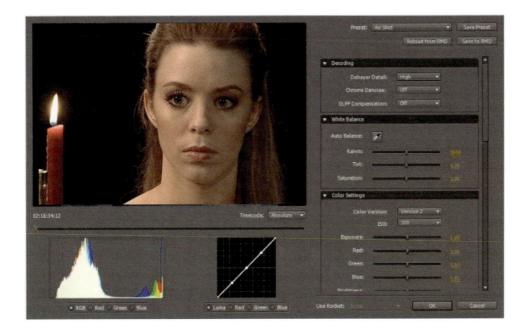

Changing Video Resolution Means Faster Preview Rendering

However, this doesn't fix dropped frame errors

You probably know that changing the screen resolution from Full (highest quality) to one-half or one-quarter reduces the amount of time that you spend rendering because Premiere only needs to display 50 or 25 percent of the total frames in your video per second. This decreases the load on the CPU and allows it to play more effects in real time without rendering.

However, if you are getting dropped frame errors, changing the resolution won't help, because the amount of data needed per second from your hard disk doesn't change as screen resolution changes.

(Continued)

21

Dropped frames can also be the result of the computer not being able to keep up with processing the frames and the effects fast enough. Setting screen playback resolution to one-half effectively quarters the amount of pixels that need to be computed. This can reduce dropped frames if the bottleneck in continuous playback is processor-related, as opposed to simply video decoding.

Premiere Now Has Stop Lights

Green is good, yellow is, ah, not so good—and both are hiding!

Both the Source and Program monitors have a small green light—called the "Dropped Frame Indicator"—just to the right of the timecode display.

When things are going great, this light stays green. However, if your system starts dropping frames, the light goes yellow. This can be caused by a hard disk that's too slow or a processor that can't compute effects fast enough in real time. When you roll your cursor over the light, a tooltip will pop up, indicating how many frames were dropped.

This is actually very important. You never want your system dropping frames, especially when you are capturing from tape, or outputting to tape, because it means that your masters will be messed up.

If this light flashes yellow, **stop!** what you are doing and figure out the problem and fix it before you get into deeper trouble.

The light itself will reset the next time you start playback.

Note: This indicator is off by default. Turn it on from the Settings menu (the wrench) in the lower right corner of the Source or Program monitor by selecting: **Show Dropped Frame Indicator**.

Use Audio Timecode for DSLR Video

Use audio timecode when merging with DSLR video

Most DSLR cameras don't record timecode; instead, they record time-of-day in place of timecode. This can be a problem when creating a merged clip, in which you marry the audio recorded on a digital recorder with the video recorded on the DSLR camera.

With Premiere CS6, you can set the timecode of a merged clip to use the timecode from an audio clip rather than default to the video timecode. This is especially useful when shooting music videos and you want to make sure that you are editing video that matches up to a particular section of the music.

Fixing Dropped Frame Errors

Dropped frames errors generally mean hard disk or CPU problems

Dropped frame errors are generally caused by one of these factors:

- A hard disk that's too slow to keep up with the video format you are editing

- A boot disk with insufficient free space

- A media disk with insufficient free space

- A hard disk that's overly fragmented, or with confused disk directories

- An effect that's too complex for the CPU to calculate in real time

- Insufficient RAM for the size of the project

- A video format (such as H.264) that's too complex for the computer to decode in real time

(Continued)

An earlier tip discussed data rates of popular video formats. Demanding more data from your storage than it is capable of delivering is the most frequent cause of dropped frames.

Try to keep at least 20 percent free space, or more, on all hard disks, because the more full a hard disk gets, the slower it goes. When a hard drive is 100 percent full, it is generally not able to either record or play back data.

Generally, defragmenting your hard drive is not something that needs to be done often, especially not with the size and speeds of hard drives today. By contrast, if other remedies have failed, defragging is worth trying.

On Macintosh systems a very useful maintenance procedure that should be done weekly is a Safe Boot, which is described in a separate tip.

The Safe Boot Procedure

A weekly maintenance procedure for Macintosh systems

Here is a three-step maintenance procedure for your Macs that will help prevent problems:

1. Start, or restart, your computer system holding the Shift key down. Continue holding the Shift key for fifteen seconds after you see the spinning gear, or a thermometer, appear during startup.

2. When startup is complete, login and go to **Utilities > Disk Utility**, select your boot drive, and click the "Repair Permissions" button.

3. When permissions repair is complete, restart your computer holding no keys down.

Pressing the Shift key during startup turns off all third-party software, all automatic software launches, and much of the operating system. It also reloads

(*Continued*)

the list of files stored on your boot disk into a special place of system memory called the "cache." For reasons that are not your fault, this cache gets corrupted and needs to be replaced. The most obvious sign of a corrupted cache is the Spinning Beach Ball of Death.

Most Mac software uses permissions to allow all the different files within the program to talk to each other. Sometimes—and, again, this isn't your fault—those permissions become corrupted. Disk Utility allows you to reset them to their factory defaults.

Restarting the computer returns your system back to normal, all buffed and polished and ready to continue work.

I recommend doing a Safe Boot whenever:

- You have a crash
- You've upgraded the operating system
- You've upgraded an application
- On Tuesdays, after lunch.

In other words, make this a regular part of your computer maintenance routine.

CHAPTER 2

Adobe Story

The Three Main Views

Projects, authoring, and the welcome screen

There are three principle views in Adobe Story:

- Project view

- Authoring view

- Welcome screen

There are lots of dialogs and panels, but everything starts with these three views. (Okay, yes, there's also the Home/Help view, but I'm not counting it.)

Project view lists the collections of documents that are needed for any production, including scripts, research, lists, schedules, and reports. This is the general organizational window for the entire application.

Authoring view is where you create, modify, review, and annotate individual scripts, schedules, and production reports.

Schedule view, which is a subset of Authoring view, is similar to a spreadsheet, where you track all the different data that you need to think about for

(Continued)

production. You access this view by double-clicking a schedule. This view is traditionally called a stripboard.

The active window, or document, is displayed with orange text in the Project view.

Customize the Project View

Make changes by clicking, twirling, and dragging

There are a variety of ways to customize the project window:

- Change the width of a column by dragging the vertical dividing line between column headers.

- Change the order of the columns by dragging the column header.

- Click the downward-pointing arrow at the extreme right side of the column headers and check, or uncheck, the columns you want to display as part of the Project view.

- Click the word "Project" on the left side of the window (the one with the downward pointing arrow) to reveal more settings.

Note: Anywhere you see an arrow, click it and something interesting will appear. Clicking arrows never deletes anything, so feel free to click away!

Restore Deleted Documents

The only thing better than ice cream and apple pie is recovering a deleted document

Poof! It's gone ... except, suddenly, you realize that you deleted the wrong document. (Yeah, I know *that* feeling all too well.) Fortunately, for those of us who are still mortal, Adobe provided a way to recover from disaster. You can undelete a document.

(Continued)

Note: When you delete a Project it is permanently deleted. Projects contain documents. While we can't recover the container Project, we can recover the documents that were inside the Project; these are much more valuable.

When you delete a Project, the contents of the project are moved to the Deleted Items section. This means that you can restore the contents of the deleted project to any existing project. (If you want to restore the contents to a project with the same name as the deleted project, first create a project with that name.)

Here's how to recover deleted files:

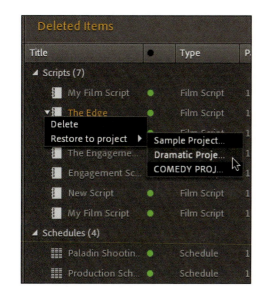

- In the Projects view, click **Deleted** in the lower-left corner of the panel. This displays a list of all deleted documents.

- Select the item, or items, that you want to restore.

- Click the small arrow to the left of the item.

- Select **Restore To Project**.

- Select the project to which you want to restore the item.

- Done.

Two Versions—Two Options

Story free is not the same as story plus

There are two versions of Story: Story Free, which is browser-based, and Story Plus, which is a desktop application.

Story Free is a free version of Story that allows you to work on projects that have been shared with you but not to create projects that others can collaborate on.

(Continued)

Story Plus allows you to create and share documents with others, as well as providing a wealth of planning and scheduling options. Story Plus also allows you to work either online or offline with your documents.

What the Heck Is this Little Green Light?

Relax. Green is good

If you are running Story Free you can skip this tip, because this only applies to Story Plus. This light only shows up in the desktop application.

The small green lights next to a document means that the online version (what you share with others) is in sync with the offline version (the copy you keep on your local computer). If the light is red, it means that the online version has not yet been stored locally—which Story will do automatically, the next time you connect online.

Keeping documents in sync means that if you have a local copy of Story (which is only available to Story Plus users), you can work on your scripts without being connected to the Internet. The next time you log into Story, the software will automatically sync the two versions.

Cool.

Organize Your Projects Into Categories

Categories can be subjects, clients, or seasons

Although optional, organizing projects into categories helps you manage your projects efficiently. Categories contain Projects. Projects contain documents, such as scripts and schedules.

(Continued)

For example, you can create a category for each of your clients, and add projects related to them in their respective category.

To create a new category:

1 Display the Project view.

2 From the left side, select **Projects > New Category**.

3 Enter the name of the category.

To add a project to a category, drag the project from the Project menu to the Category on the left to which you want to add the project.

How to Share a Project

Sharing is how you allow your team to collaborate

Sharing a project with others requires Story Plus. To share a project, select it in the Project view, and click the Share icon in the toolbar in the upper right section of the screen.

This displays the Share Project window. Add the e-mail for someone you want to share all projects files with (and check the "Send E-mail Notification" checkbox at the bottom if you want them alerted via e-mail).

Then, from the popup menu, select the access privileges that you want them to have:

- Coauthor means they can comment and make changes to documents.

- Reviewer means they can make comments but not make changes.

- Reader means they can read all the documents but not make comments or changes.

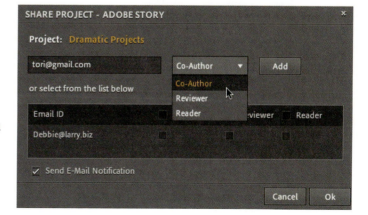

(Continued)

You can change their status at any time, as well as remove someone from the list whom you no longer want to have access to project files.

More Things to Do With Projects

Here's how to rename and delete stuff

To remove a project from a category, select it, click the arrow to the left of the category name and select **Remove from Category**. This does NOT delete the project.

Note: If you delete a project from the All Projects list, the project is deleted from all the categories to which it belongs.

To rename a category, double-click the category name.

To delete a category, select the category you want to delete and select **Projects > Delete** from the menu in the top left corner.

Archive Projects

Just because you don't need it doesn't mean you don't need it

You can archive projects that you do not use frequently. The archived projects are hidden from view but are still available.

To archive a project:

❶ Select the project name in the Projects view.

❷ Click the arrow to the left of the project.

❸ Select **Archive**.

(*Continued*)

Two things happen: the project instantly disappears from the project list. DON'T PANIC—it isn't erased, but it is hidden. The other, which you can't see yet, is that its icon changed.

To display archived projects, check the **Show Archived** checkbox at the bottom left of the window to display the archived projects. You can identify archived projects from their icon.

To restore an archived project, make sure that all archived projects are showing. Then:

● Select the project in the Projects view.

● Click the arrow to the left of the project.

● Select **Restore**. The icon changes to reflect its restored status.

Save Your Work—Automatically

Story has a built-in auto save feature

Adobe Story has a built-in Auto Save function that automatically saves your work every five minutes. To change this, or turn it off:

● Open a script

● Select **Edit > Properties**

● Click **Auto Save**

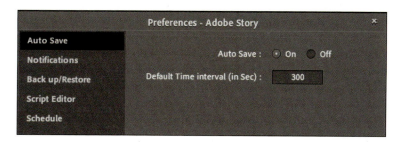

Note: For those of us who are mathematically challenged, the Default Time interval of 300 seconds equals five minutes. If you want to save your work every ten minutes, set this to **600**.

Back Up/Restore Data

It never hurts to have copies

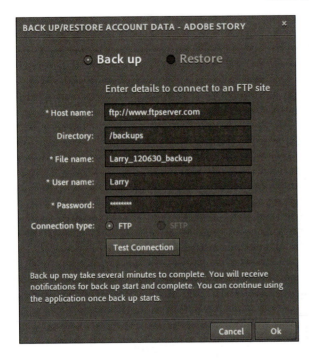

In addition to Auto Save, you can back up your data in Adobe Story to a remote site. While you can keep copies of all your documents offline on your local hard disk, you can also send copies to an FTP, or SFTP, server if you have access. Even better, if necessary, you can use the backup file created on the server to restore data.

The data that you back up includes all the files currently in Adobe Story along with their organizational information. When you restore data, the data is restored using the organizational information in the backup file.

A notification appears after every backup or restore operation informing you whether the backup or restore was successful. The notification also provides information on the location of the data that was backed up or restored. Save this somewhere, so that you know how to get your data back!

❶ In the Projects view, select **Projects > Backup/Restore**.

❷ In the Back Up/Restore Account dialog:

(a) Select whether you want to backup or restore.

(b) Enter the FTP address and log-in information (the data in this screen shot is fictitious—contact your webmaster for actual login info).

(c) Give your backup file a name. I prefer using words, rather than the string of numbers that Story suggests.

(d) If you are restoring data, enter the name of the file that you want to restore. This suggests two things: use file names that you will remember, and keep notes of what you backed up and when you backed it up.

(Continued)

❸ To test your connection, click **Test**. Although it is not required, it is always a good idea to make sure everything connects.

❹ Click **OK** to back up or restore data.

Tracking the Key Creative Team

Enter team members once, track forever

You can enter key members of your team once per project, then have them added automatically to every script and report.

Open your script, and select **Edit > Script Properties**.

In the lower left corner, click the **Edit Production Information** button.

Enter the names of your key creative team members. You can even save them to reuse on future projects by clicking the Create button.

Note: You can also do this by clicking the gear icon next to the project name.

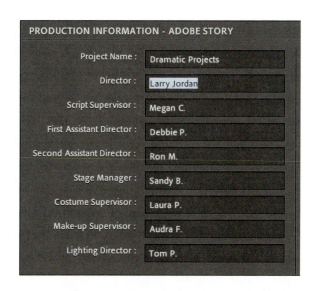

There Are Four Types of Scripts

Pick the script template that best matches what you want to create

There are four script templates in Story:

● Film Script

● TV Script

● AV Script

● Multicolumn Scripts

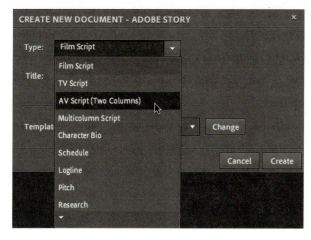

(*Continued*)

Each of these is a template designed to match current industry formats for layout, fonts, and pagination.

Select the format you want, give it a name, select a template, and get to work.

Scripts are automatically added to the project that was active when you created the script.

Change The Look of Your Script

You can quickly change the template without changing any text

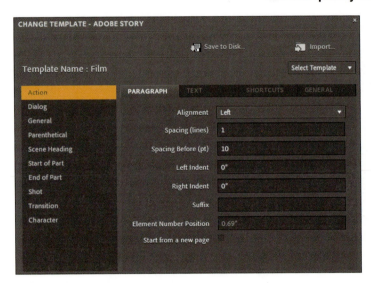

For TV and film scripts, you can modify an existing script template or change to a different template. For example, you can change formatting, text style, keyboard shortcuts, and text automation.

Note: Not all templates have multiple versions, but all templates can be modified.

To change the template for a film or TV script:

❶ In the script view, select **Edit > Template**.

❷ To modify a template, select a setting on the left and change a parameter by clicking any of the four tabs across the top.

❸ To change a template, select a new style from the Select Template pop-up menu near the top right corner.

Note: You can also change the font used in the template. Go to **Edit > Template** and click the **Text** tab. However, professional script readers expect all scripts

(Continued)

to be written in Courier, which is the default font in Story. Be cautious when changing fonts if you are submitting your script to a professional reader.

Adding Script Properties

A fast way to properly track your scripts

Need to track things like Script ID, episode titles, or episode numbers? Use the Script Properties.

Open your script, then select **Edit > Script Properties**.

Script Properties

Script ID	The Engagement
Transmission Date	Feb 28, 2012
Episode Number	The Engagement
Episode Title	The Engagement
Notes	

Edit Production Information...   Cancel   Save

Make a Comment

You can add comments to just about anything

See that balloon symbol on the right side of a document? Click it and you can add a comment.

Comments can be added to just about anything, including many reports.

This is an ideal way for creative team members to ask questions without messing with the content of the script or report.

Review All Comments

Making a comment doesn't help if you can't review it

Story makes it easy to see all of the comments associated with a particular script or document. To open the Comment panel, select **View > Comments**.

To jump to a comment, click on the Comment in the Comments panel.

Comments can be searched, sorted, and deleted.

INT. RESTAURANT -- DAY

THREE PEOPLE IN THEIR 20'S ARE AT A
TABLE IN A CASUAL RESTAURANT. WE HEAR
CROWD NOISE AND THE SOUND OF EATING.
THE LIGHTING IS ROSY, THE DINERS ARE
HAPPY. IT IS EARLY EVENING.

DANIELLE:

shoot this in limbo so we imply a crowd without actually HIRING a crowd.
Larry ...rdan Feb 28, 2012 10:34 PM

Make this late afternoon.
Larry ...rdan Feb 28, 2012 10:35 PM

Track Script Changes

Tracking changes shows who's messing with your immortal words

Story allows you to track changes in your documents similar to what you would do in Microsoft Word.

To turn on change tracking, go to **Review > Start Tracking Changes**.

Then, change something and watch what happens.

To turn off change tracking, go back to the Review menu and uncheck it.

> *Note*: Only the original author of a document can turn on change tracking. Coauthors can make and accept changes. Reviewers can see changes. Readers can only see documents in their original, unchanged, state.

Tag Production Elements in the Script

Adding production elements simplifies tracking people and things later

To add key personnel to a project, such as director, script supervisor, lighting, and so on, click the downward-pointing arrow next to the project name and select **Production Information**.

To add scene elements to a script, select **View > Scene Properties Panel**. Here you can adjust the scene time, detect nonspeaking characters, edit the running time, locations, and shot lists, and more.

This tagging panel has many options. Read the Help files to learn the details.

How to Add or Remove An Act

Acts allow you to easily organize your longer scripts

To add an act:

1 Place your cursor in a scene that you want to make the first scene of the new act. The end of the act is either the beginning of the next act or the end of script if there are no other acts after the inserted act.

2 Select **Edit > Insert Act/Part Break**.

Note: You can only insert an act in a scene that is not the first scene of an act.

To remove an act:

1 Place the cursor in the first scene of the act you want to remove.

2 Select **Edit > Remove Act #**.

Outline View

A faster way to review and navigate

Outline view provides an outline of your script by scene. This is a fast way to see all the scenes in your script and jump between them.

You can selectively display one or more of the following in the script view:

1 Show outline view.

2 Expand scenes in outline view.

3 Show scene property panel.

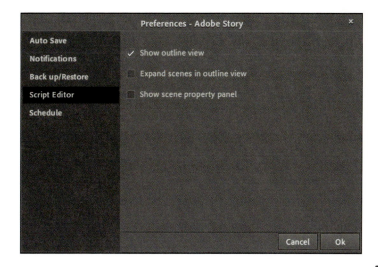

(Continued)

To toggle the display of Outline View:

❶ With a script open, select **Edit > Preferences**.

❷ In the Preferences dialog, select **Script Editor**.

❸ This allows you to display:

(a) Outline view.

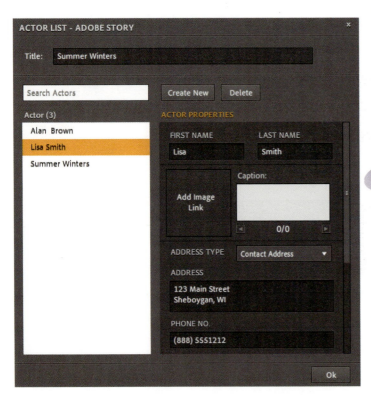

(b) Expanding the scenes in Outline view to see the unformatted script text for the start of the scene.

(c) Show the scene property panel where you can specify a wide variety of scene specific information.

Note: New or changed settings take place after you close and reopen a script.

Using Actor Lists

This is a fast way to keep track of everyone you need on camera

Create a contact list of all your actors using an Actor List. Select the Project you want to add actors to, then, select Manage Lists from the upper right toolbar.

Create a new actor and enter contact information. To edit an actor, select their name, and change the displayed information. To delete an actor, select their name and click Delete.

Reading the Lights

These dots are a fast way to see who's in a scene

When your script is open, look to the left where the word "Outline" appears. Underneath the Outline header is a list of all the scenes in your script.

Click the scene name, and the unformatted text of your script appears.

Next to the name of the scene are a series of colored dots; Adobe calls these "character dots." Each dot represents a character in your script. (In this case, the bright pink dot represents the character "Lisa.")

These small dots allow you to quickly see which characters are in a scene.

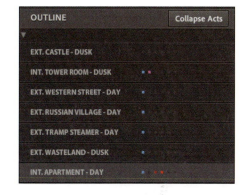

Disable Characters

"He's dead, Jim."

You've been in a writing frenzy, inventing plot, characters, and incredible dialog. Hmmm ... some of it is too incredible. Delete, delete, delete.

Except, now, you've got characters showing up in the "Auto-Complete List" that you no longer need. Time to disable those pesky critters.

To disable a character:

● Open a script so it displays in Script view.

● Select **Edit > Character List**.

● Scroll to the bottom and check **Disable Character**.

This removes the character from all lists but won't delete the character if you've used it in a script.

To enable a character, display this same menu, select the character name and uncheck "Disable Character."

Note: You can also delete dead sets using the **Edit > Set List** option.

Adding Nonspeaking Characters

Keeping track of people who can't speak for themselves

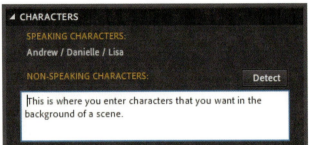

Many times in a scene, you want other characters to appear, even though they are not talking. Open the script you want to add characters into. Select **View > Scene Properties Panel**. Then, twirl down the arrow next to **Characters**.

If you have already listed the characters in the scene, click the Detect button to add them into the properties for that scene.

If you have not yet written them into the script, simply enter their name in the white box below the Nonspeaking Characters title. This allows Story to track characters and actors to add them to production reports, call sheets, and so on as you get closer to production.

Validate Sets and Characters

This is even better than checking their ID!

Story Plus has the option to validate character and set names. This allows to you see if the character or set you are writing about exists in either the character list or the set list. If so, great. If not, you can quickly add them to the appropriate list.

● Open a script so it displays in Script view.

● Enter any characters in the script, either speaking or nonspeaking, that are not already part of your character list. Make sure you add them using the Character keyboard shortcut or pop-up menu.

(Continued)

- Select **Edit > Validate Character Names**.

- In the New Characters dialog, select the names you want to add to the character list and click **OK**. Story displays a message indicating the characters were added to the list.

This technique works for both speaking and nonspeaking actors. (This isn't an issue for sets as, generally, sets don't speak.)

Note: If all the characters in your script are already part of your character list, Story will display a message indicating that fact.

Assign Dialog Numbers

Help your actors keep track of their lines

Numbering paragraphs of dialog can help your actors and production team make sure everything you need gets recorded. With Story, you can create sequential dialog numbers automatically, reset the numbering with each new script page, and even delete dialog numbers. Here's how.

To assign dialog numbers:

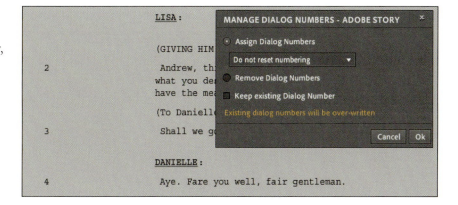

1 Open a script so that it is displayed in Authoring view and select **Production > Manage Dialog Numbers**.

2 Select **Assign Dialog Numbers**.

❸ If desired, choose one of the following options from the pop-up dialog:

(a) **Reset numbering on new page:** Story resets the dialog number to 1 on every new page

(b) **Reset numbering on new scene:** Story resets the dialog number to 1 with start of every new scene

❹ If you are making changes to an existing script, select **Keep Existing Dialog Number**. With this option, existing dialog numbers are left undisturbed and new dialogs are numbered alphabetically with the previous existing dialog's number as a prefix. For example, if you insert two dialogs following scene number 3, they are numbered as 3A and 3B.

Export Report to MS Word

A fast and easy way to move files between applications

Now you can export your reports to an MS Word-compatible .htm format.

To export a report to Word:

● From the Projects window, open a report so that you can see it displayed.

● Select **File > Export As > HTM - MS® Word Compatible (.htm)** and save the report to your computer.

● Right click the file and choose to open the file with MS Word. For best results, view the report file in the Print Layout mode.

You can manipulate the report just like any other word document.

(Continued)

The reason for right-clicking to select Word, is that the .HTM format can be read by many different applications and double-clicking the document will open it in a web browser.

Note: The column resize option in Word only works for individual pages and not for the whole report.

Add Script Changes Made Elsewhere

It is easy to incorporate script changes made in other applications

You thought the script was done, so you exported it to Word to print and share with the world. Except ... well, there was that one scene that could use a tweak. So, you tweaked it. And now, you've got two versions of the script in two different applications.

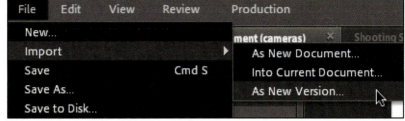

When you edit a copy of a script outside Adobe Story, such as Word or Final Draft, you can import the document as the latest version of the script. This means that you don't need to make all those corrections again, manually.

For screenplays, film scripts, and TV scripts, you can import a script as the latest version of a script. You can import the following document types: TXT, PDF, CSV, Final Draft and Movie Magic scheduling, and RTF.

What happens is that the newly imported version becomes the current script in Story. The script that was current in Story before the import, becomes the latest member of your script archives.

To import a file as current version of a document:

(Continued)

1 Open a script to display it in Authoring view.

2 Select **File > Import > As New Version**.

3 Navigate to a supported file and select it.

Once imported, the new script behaves just like any other script created in Story.

Add Images to Characters, Actors, and Sets

It is a whole lot easier to show than explain

Did you know that you can add images to characters, actors, and sets? As long as the image can be found online, it's easy. Here's how.

To add an image to an actor, character, or set list:

● Go online and locate the image you want to add.

● Copy the web address of the image from the browser address bar.

● Go to the Projects view and click the **Manage Lists** button in the toolbar at the top of the screen.

● Select the List to which you want to add the image.

● Click **Add Image Link** inside the square placeholder.

● In the Manage Images dialog, click **Add Image Link** inside the square placeholder.

● In the Image Link dialog, paste the link and click **OK**.

● If you want, type a caption for the image.

● To add more images, click the **Add Image Link** button at the bottom of the Manage Images dialog. You can have multiple images associated with the same list item.

Add Storyboard Images

Illustrate your script with images

Storyboards are images that illustrate key moments in your script. And, as such, they become a property in scripts. You can view and manage Storyboards from the Scene Properties panel. In the Storyboards field, you can add one or more storyboard images for a scene.

Storyboards are also visible in the schedule. Any discrepancy between the storyboards in the schedule and the relevant scripts are flagged in the Sync dialog.

Here's how to add storyboard images:

❶ Open a script so it is displayed in the Authoring view.

- Select the title of the scene in the script.

- Then, select **Edit > Scene Properties Panel**, or right-click the text and select **Storyboard**.

- At the top of Scene Properties or in the Manage Images dialog, click **Add Image Link** inside the square placeholder.

- In the Image Link dialog, paste the link to the online image and click **OK**.

- If you want, type a caption for the image.

- To add more images, click the **Add Image Link** button at the bottom of the Manage Images dialog.

Sync Scripts to Schedules

Syncing shouldn't require thinking ...

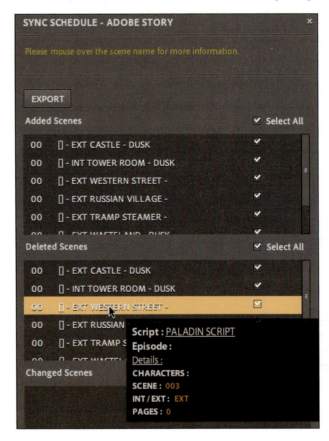

The whole goal of preproduction is to find a way to craft a story that can be told using pictures and sound. That means that we need to do more than just write the script, we need to connect that script to a production schedule.

Then, we need to keep the two in sync as the planning evolves. And that is a lot easier to say than to do. Story is here to help because scripts change all the time.

When you select scenes or scripts in Adobe Story for scheduling, Adobe Story automatically creates a schedule using information in those scripts. Some of the things that you can do with a schedule include:

- Add banners and breaks.

- Sort the schedule by actors, characters, sets, or any of **64** criteria!

- Split the schedule across days

- Save the schedule to disk

- Rearrange the script in shooting order

To keep scripts and schedules together, you sync them. Syncing tells the schedule to reorganize itself based on the latest iteration of the script. You can retain some of the data in the schedule during the sync. You can select the properties to sync. The properties you do not select are not synced, which means the existing data in the schedule is left untouched.

(Continued)

To sync a schedule:

- Display a schedule in the Schedule view and click **Sync** from the top toolbar.

- In the Sync Schedule dialog, select the revised scenes that you want to sync; or uncheck what you don't want to sync. To sync tags, select **Sync Tags**.

- To selectively sync properties of the revised scenes, click **Select Properties To Update**.

Note: Scheduling, syncing changes in a script into a schedule, production reports, and script compare are only available to Story Plus users.

Compare Schedules

How to avoid being in two places at the same time

Story allows you to compare two schedules and find out if any sets or characters are committed to both schedules at the same time. If you find any conflicts, you can adjust the schedules to fix them.

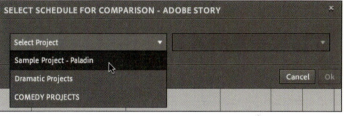

Here's how to compare two schedules:

1. Open the first schedule you want to compare with another schedule and click **Compare** from the toolbar at the top.

2. In the Select Schedule For Comparison dialog, select the relevant project and schedule for comparison.

Story displays the Compare Schedules dialog and lists the conflicts, if any. Also, you can see the schedule, day, and time where the resource conflict exists.

Note: Although you will need to make any corrections manually, you can easily use this to review potential conflicts with people or scenes.

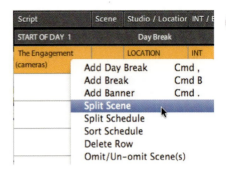

How to Split Scenes

A split scene is a scene that will be shot across more than one day

How to split a scene:

● Open the production report that contains the scene you want to split.

● Right-click the name of a scene and from the pop-up menu, select **Split Scene**.

The strip is split into two. You can add schedule notes to clarify that a scene will be shot over multiple days.

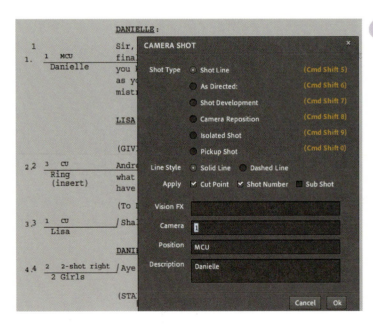

Add Camera Shots

Adding shots to the script during preproduction speeds production

Adding camera shots to the script allows better planning of camera angles, story visualization, and saves time later when you need to create shot sheets.

To add a camera shot, open the script you want to use. Put the cursor where you want the shot change to occur and select **Production > Camera shot** (shortcut: **Shift+Command+C / Shift+Cntrl+C**).

In the resulting dialog, fill in the various pieces of information the camera operator will need to get the shot.

Create Camera Card Reports

Story can generate camera cards, or shot sheets, for all cameras

A camera card report (or shot sheet) is a list of all shots for a particular camera in the order the shots need to be taken. In order to generate camera cards, you first need to assign camera shots to various lines in the script. This involves going line-by-line through the script and then creating a camera card report:

1 Do one of the following:

    (a) In the Project view, click **Reports**.

    (b) In the Schedule view, click **Reports**.

2 In the Reports dialog, do the following and click **Generate**:

    (a) Specify if you want to create report for all the cameras or a specific camera.

    (b) If you want to include videotape elements in the report, select **Include VTs**.

    (c) If you are generating a report from the Project view, select **Select All Documents** or one of the schedules. Camera cards cannot be created from more than one production schedule.

Camera Shot Card			Camera No: 3	Card No: 1
SHOT	**LENS**	**POS**	**SHOT DESCRIPTION**	
			The Engagement (cameras)/ INT RESTAURANT -- LATE AFTERNOON	
1		XWS	Establish	
5		CU	Ring (insert)	
8		MS zoom in	Andrew	

Resize Report Columns

Easily change the widths of report columns

Now you can resize the columns in a report just by dragging a column boundary. If you are dragging in a report, Story displays the readjusted width of the column in inches. For reports that extend beyond one page, adjusting the column width in one page changes the column width on all the pages.

To resize columns:

● Hover the mouse over a column boundary. When the cursor changes in shape to a double-pointing arrow, right-click and drag the boundary to readjust the column width.

Note: Column headers are located above report fields, in the gray area at the top of the screen. Dragging column dividers inside the report won't work. I know; I've tried.

Change Text in Report

Need to change the text in a report field? Easy!

Need to change the contents of a column header in a report, or modify a record? It's easy—open the report and double-click the field that you want to change.

One of two things will happen:

● The text in the header becomes available for editing.

● The Strip Properties panel appears, where you can change both the name of the column header, as well as see and modify all the text associated with that record.

To record your changes, tab, or click, to another record.

Changing Start Times in the Production Report

Make manual changes in scene start time

By default, the start time (S. Start) of an entry in the Production Report is same as the end of the previous line (S. End). You can manually change the start time of an entry by double-clicking the duration and entering your own number.

To remove these manual changes, click **Recalc** in the toolbar at the top of the screen.

Alert the Media!

Add an information-only banner to a schedule

You can add an information-only banner to a schedule to make announcements. An information-only banner supports text.

To add a banner:

① In a schedule, select the row *under* which you want to add the banner.

② Select **Edit > Add Banner (No Duration)**.

③ Edit the banner info to add a message/announcement.

To remove a banner, click the small "x" at the extreme right-side of the banner.

Print a Schedule

Schedules can be printed to either paper or PDF.

Once a production schedule is created for a script, and production elements are added to the schedule, you can create a variety of reports.

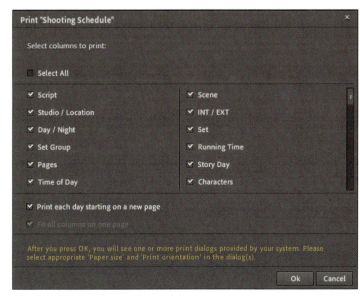

(Continued)

To print a schedule:

1 Double-click a schedule in the Projects window to display it.

2 With the schedule displayed, select **File > Print**.

3 In the Print dialog, you can:

(a) Select the columns you want to print. By default, all the columns currently displayed in the schedule view are selected. Scroll down to see all available columns to print.

(b) Select **Print each day starting on a new page**. This option prints separate days' schedule on separate pages. Adobe Story prints the day breaks on bottom of the pages, starting each of the next days' schedule on new pages.

(c) Select **Fit all columns on one page**. This squeezes all your columns, but not your rows, to fit on one page. Landscape is best in this situation, but even medium-sized schedules will become an eyechart.

These schedules and reports are, essentially, spreadsheets. They will look best when printed in landscape mode.

Favorite Keyboard Shortcuts

Here are some of my favorite keyboard shortcuts for Story.

What it Does	Shortcut	Menu
apply scene heading	Ctrl+1 / Cmd+1	Scene Element Menu
apply action	Ctrl+2 / Cmd+2	Scene Element Menu
apply character	Ctrl+3 / Cmd+3	Scene Element Menu
apply parenthetical	Ctrl+4 / Cmd+4	Scene Element Menu
apply dialog	Ctrl+5 / Cmd+5	Scene Element Menu
apply transition	Ctrl+6 / Cmd+6	Scene Element Menu
apply shot	Ctrl+7 / Cmd+7	Scene Element Menu
apply general	Ctrl+8 / Cmd+8	Scene Element Menu
introduce new line	Shift+Enter	
page break	Ctrl+Enter	
next scene	Ctrl+Shift+J / Cmd+Shift+J	Edit > Jump > Next Scene
previous scene	Ctrl+Shift+K / Cmd+Shift+K	Edit > Jump > Prev Scene
go to next element in script	Cntrl+J / Cmd+J	Edit > Jump > Next Element
go to previous element	Ctrl+K / Cmd+K	Edit > Jump > Prev Element
switch between Authoring and Project views	Ctrl+~ [tilde]	

CHAPTER 3

Adobe Prelude CS6

Adobe Prelude CS6 is brand new. It is designed to review, ingest, log, select, and export tapeless media files for use by Premiere Pro CS6, or Final Cut Pro 7. The advantage of Prelude is that one person can be reviewing and selecting footage while a second person is editing the selected footage.

Keep in mind that Prelude is designed for tapeless media; you would not use it to capture media from video tape.

Naming Your Source Media Folders

A helpful system for naming folders

The first rule when working with tapeless media is to copy the entire contents of the card to your hard disk *before* ingesting. That way, you have a complete backup of the card. (Maintaining the complete folder structure as created by the camera is very important when working with tapeless media, such as AVCHD.)

However, equally important is that you name your media folders something that helps you figure out what's inside. For that purpose, here's the system I use myself:

- Create a *Source Media* folder on a second hard drive, not the boot disk.

- Inside Source Media, create a folder for each client or series.

- Inside the Client folder, create a folder for each project.

I tend to favor a two-letter, two-number combination for my project code—where the letters represent the client and the numbers represent the specific job for that client.

Then, inside the project folder, I create a folder for each camera card that I'm going to copy to my computer. Each folder has a very specific naming convention:

- Project code

- The date the material was shot

- Which camera shot it (A camera, B camera, C camera, etc.)

- The number for card recorded for that camera on that day (first card, second card, third card, etc.)

Here's an example of a typical folder name: **JM02-120928-A01**

Project Files Don't Store Media

They just point to the media on your hard drive

When you create a project file, you aren't actually storing any media in the project file itself. Instead, you are collecting a list of file paths and file names that point to where media is stored on your hard disk.

This is why thinking about file organization while copying and naming media on your hard disk is so important. This is also why moving media, after you have ingested and logged it in Prelude, creates such a mess.

(Continued)

Because Prelude is simply creating lists of file locations—very fancy lists, I might add—thinking through where you want to store media and how you want folders named *before* using Prelude will save a ton of time trying to find and organize files later.

Files Gone Missing? Relink Them

Relinking allows you to reconnect files that have moved or changed file names

This feature is new with the 1.01 update. Relinking allows you to reconnect to clips that Prelude is unable to locate.

When Prelude initially starts, it verifies that all of the clips contained in a project can be located. If it can't find a clip, it flags them and displays a dialog asking what you want to do. You can decide not to link to them—for example, you trashed a bunch of files that you no longer need. Or, you can decide to relink them.

If you say "Yes" to relinking, Prelude opens a dialog box so that you can navigate to where they are located. (Notice the full path and file name are displayed at the top of this dialog.)

Note: To save you time, if all the missing files are in the same location, when you find and link to the first file, Prelude will automatically link to the rest of them.

Note: As of this release, Adobe does not provide a way to relink missing clips contained in a rough cut. (A better option is to relink the source clips in the project.) This is also true for subclips.

J-K-L Keyboard Shortcuts Also Work in Prelude

These three shortcuts make playback and review faster

Prelude adopts a set of keyboard shortcuts common to many editing applications for fast playback and review.

Press:

> **J** to go backward
>
> **K** to stop
>
> **L** to go forward

Press **J** twice to rewind at double speed, or press **L** twice to go forward at double speed. Anything that makes an application faster is okay in my book!

Missing Workspace Elements

Not all panels are visible all the time

Are you missing tabs—which Adobe calls "panels"—in your workspace?

You can find them under the Window menu. (There you will find things like Audio Master Meters, Events, History, Metadata, and Timecode.)

Tabs that are not checked are currently hidden. Tabs that are checked are displayed in the current workspace.

Customizing a Workspace

Custom workspaces allow you to create a workspace that works for you

One of the great features in all Adobe products is their ability to create a custom workspace—then save it for future use.

(Continued)

From the Window menu, select a panel that you want to add to the interface. That panel is now displayed as a floating window.

Grab the tab inside the floating window and drag it roughly where you want it to go. As you drag the tab around the interface, notice that different sections within a panel glow purple.

Once the tab is docked, you can drag it from side to side to change the order of tabs from left to right.

Here's how to decode what the placement of the purple shape means:

Purple Shape	What it Means
Shape in middle of panel	Panel tab placed at top of panel, in line with other panel tabs
Shape in header with other tabs	Panel tab placed at top of panel, in line with other panel tabs
Shape as wedge at top of panel	Panel will be placed as separate panel above the existing panel
Shape as wedge at left of panel	Panel will be placed as separate panel to left of panel
Shape as wedge at right of panel	Panel will be placed as separate panel to right of panel
Shape as wedge at bottom of panel	Panel will be placed as separate panel below the existing panel
Green indicator	When a panel is pushed to the edge of the interface to create a new frame

Save a Custom Workspace

Saving a workspace allows you to reuse it over and over

Once you have a customized workspace, you could just leave it—Prelude will remember the current workspace from one session to the next. However, a

(Continued)

much smarter option is to save the workspace, because that way, even if you reset the application, you can always return to the saved version.

First, customize the workspace as you see fit.

Then, from either the Window menu, or the Workspace popup menu, select **New Workspace**.

Give your new workspace a name and click **OK**.

It now appears in the workspace menu.

To delete a workspace, return to the same menu and select **Delete Workspace**.

Reset A Workspace

All is not lost if you totally mess up

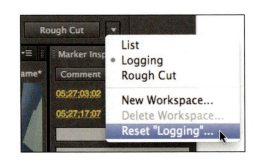

If you have been customizing your workspace and have so completely screwed it up that there is no hope for recovery, you can easily reset the workspace to its default layout.

Go to the small, downward-pointing arrow in the top right corner of the screen. It's next to Rough Cut, and select **Reset** [the name of the workspace].

A small dialog appears asking you to confirm that you want to reset the workspace. Say **Yes**, and Prelude resets the workspace to its default layout.

Selecting Files

Checking files is even better than selecting files before ingest

In order to select a file for ingest, you have to do more than just select it. You have to make sure that you click the checkbox in the lower right-hand corner. In fact, you don't need to select a file at all—the box just needs to be checked.

(Continued)

To select a file for ingest, check the corresponding checkbox in the lower right corner of each clip's icon. In the screen shot on the right, only the two checked files (on the left) will be imported. Here are some keyboard shortcuts that can help.

If you click on a clip to select it, or select a range of clips, then type the letter **V**, the checkbox will be toggled. V toggles checkboxes on or off for all selected clips. (Remember, clips must be checked to be imported.)

If you want to check all the clips, whether selected or not, use **Shift+V**.

If you want to uncheck all the clips, use **Control+Shift+V**.

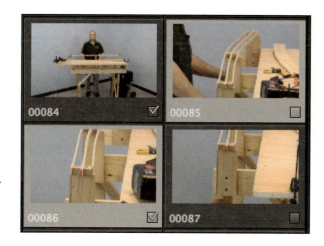

When Ingesting, Prelude Creates Reference Files

By default, prelude just creates pointers to show where source media is located

Prelude does not store media within its project file. Instead, it points to where the media is stored on your hard drive.

This means that Prelude project files are very small. However, it also means that when you share your Prelude project with, say, Premiere, the Premiere editor will need to have access to the same files on the same path.

There are two ways to see where your source files are stored:

- Right-click a file name in the Project Browser and select **Reveal in Finder**.

- Select **Window > Metadata** to view the entire file path name in the Metadata window.

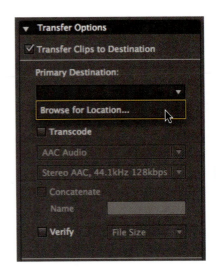

When Should You Specify a Destination?

Destinations are not needed when working with native video formats

A destination is where a copy of your media is stored. Destinations are *only* necessary when you are transcoding into different formats, or ingesting partial clips.

A "native" video format is the source video format shot by the camera. Different cameras use different video formats. Whatever format the camera shot is its "native" format.

Note: To "transcode" media means to convert it from one format to another.

When you are working with media in its camera-native format, you are simply ingesting *references* to media that is stored on your hard disk. You are only creating pointers to existing media. So, no destination is necessary because no copies are being made.

However, when you ingest partial clips, or create multiple versions of the same clip, or transcode a clip into a different format—all of which generate new media in addition to the original source file—you need to specify where that new media will be stored.

Note: In order to ingest a partial clip, transcoding must be turned on.

Set a Destination to Store Transcoded Files

Destinations are required when transcoding clips, or capturing portions of clips

Whenever you ingest a partial clip or need to convert it from one video codec to another, you need to transcode and set a destination.

(Continued)

One of the cool features in Prelude is that you can set multiple destinations, for example to create both proxy files and master files at the same time. To do so, check the **Transfer Clips to Destination** checkbox at the top of the Transfer Options on the right side of the screen.

Click the **Browse for Location** pop-up menu under Primary Destination and set it to a second drive. It is generally recommended not to use the boot disk as a location.

If you want to create multiple versions of the ingested file, create a second destination, or as many additional destinations as you need.

Set In and Out Before Ingest

Save disk space, just capture the portion of the clips you need

You can capture just the portions of the clips you need by setting an In and an Out for a clip before you ingest it. To do so, open the Ingest workspace and navigate to the clips you want to ingest.

Click in the image of a clip you want to ingest and slide your cursor near the bottom of the image. As you drag across the clip, you can preview the image.

When you find the spot you want to start, type **I** to set the In. When you find the place you want to end, type **O** to set the Out.

Now, when you ingest the clip, only the portion between the In and the Out will be ingested.

Note: Ingesting a partial clip requires that it be transcoded.

Verify What You Ingest

It's always good to know that you got what you wanted

When you are ingesting whole clips, you can verify that everything was safely ingested by clicking the **Verify** button at the bottom of Transfer Options.

When checked, this will verify the accuracy of the copy based on either file size or a file checksum.

This option is only available when you are copying entire clips. If **Transfer Clips to Destination** is not checked or if you are capturing partial clips, this option is not available.

In general, when this option is available, it is a good idea to check it. A little extra double-checking doesn't hurt.

Be Careful What You Delete

Deleting the wrong thing won't hurt, but it will cost you time

When you delete a clip reference in the Project Library, you are not deleting any media on your hard disk; you are simply deleting the reference to the media that is displayed in the Project Library.

However, once you delete the reference, the only way you can bring the clip back is to ingest it again.

Undo won't work.

Multiple Destinations Simplify Creating Multiple Versions

Create multiple copies of the same clip all at one time

The benefit to using multiple destinations is that you are able to create, say, a low-res proxy file and a high-res master file of the same media at the same time. Or you can use Prelude in the field to make multiple copies of your camera source media to multiple hard drives at the same time.

There's no limit to the number of destinations that Prelude supports. You should always create the Primary Destination first, then, add as many secondary destinations as you need versions of the same clip.

Keep in mind that adding additional copies of clips also increases the storage space required by your media.

When Should You Consider Transcoding?

Transcoding converts files from one format to another

When we transcode, we are converting media from one format to another. Transcoding is a good option when you want to standardize different media to the same image size, frame rate, scanning or codec.

Transcoding is also a good option when you want to optimize media for effects or color correction. AVCHD and H.264 are very difficult formats to edit or color correct due to the mathematics involved in their compression and the reduced color space in the format. Transcoding these formats into ProRes, DNxHD, or AVC-Intra will speed rendering and provide higher image quality for effects.

Transcoding Happens in the Background

Adobe Media Encoder does the work while you review and log clips

One of the best things about transcoding is that it happens in the background. This means that you can continue to review and log clips while, in the background, Adobe Media Encoder is converting clips from one format to another.

You can either monitor the status of this conversion by switching into Adobe Media Encoder from Prelude and checking the status screen, or you can read the next tip.

Want to Know the Status of Ingesting?

Prelude tells you at the bottom of the screen

You don't need to switch over to Adobe Media Encoder to check on the ingest status of your clips.

Just look at the bottom of the Prelude screen. It indicates the clip it is currently working on, how far along it is, and gives you the ability to pause or cancel the ingest.

Best Transcode Settings for Editing

All transcode settings are created using Adobe Media Encoder

The initial release of Prelude offered very limited transcoding settings. In fact, they were awful—all of the HD settings were designed for final web distribution or creating low-res proxies rather than master files for editing.

(Continued)

With the release of the 1.0.1 update, Adobe added additional transcoding settings for the Mac that now support ProRes. Be sure to update your system to the latest version and download these new settings from Adobe's website.

If you are on Windows, using the AVC-Intra codec will provide similar high-quality results. And added benefit of the AVC-Intra codec is that it is cross-platform. (Two other codecs worth considering are Avid DNxHD, or GoPro Cineform, both of which are available at the company's websites: www.avid.com and www.cineform.com.)

Ingesting clips in their native format is fine when you are ingesting complete clips. However, when transcoding, make sure to work with a format that edits easily and provides high quality.

Better Transcoding Options

Prelude 1.01 Adds new presets to improve transcoding

One of the problems with the initial release of Prelude was that, in order to ingest a partial clip, you needed to transcode the media. And the transcoding options provided with Prelude, which are based on presets in Adobe Media Encoder, were really poor.

New with the 1.01 release for Macintosh users are a series of new presets that improve the options for transcoding files for editing.

When looking for transcoding options, select either an SD format, a ProRes format for Mac users, or AVC-Intra for Windows users.

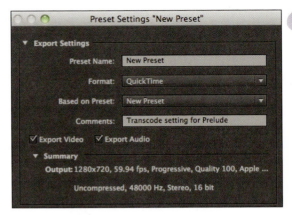

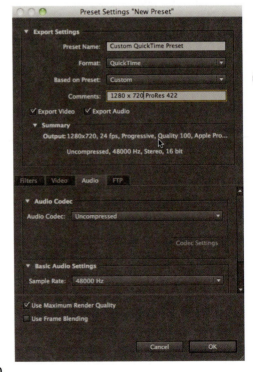

Use Adobe Media Encoder to Create Custom Transcode Settings

Prelude automatically reads all custom settings created in AME

If you want to create your own custom transcoding settings, use Adobe Media Encoder (AME).

Any compression or transcoding settings created in AME are automatically displayed in Prelude's Transcode menu options.

Note: However, as of this writing, AME does not support either audio pass-through or frame-rate pass-through. So, transcode a few files and test them in your workflow to make sure the transcoding settings will work with your project.

What Are the Best Audio Formats for Transcoding?

Uncompressed audio is better than compressed audio for editing

The default settings for audio presets in Adobe Media Encoder are highly compressed and designed for the web. These presets should be avoided for media you want to use in editing.

If all you need is the audio, select the **Waveform Audio** preset.

If you need high-quality audio and video, select the QuickTime preset. Then, click the Audio tab and set:

- Audio codec to Uncompressed
- Sample rate to 48000 Hz
- Check **Maximum Render Quality**

These settings will create .WAV files that any video editing software can use.

Adding Markers

Markers are how prelude logs and selects media

Unlike most editing software, markers in Prelude are expected to have a duration, because what you are doing is actually marking a portion of a clip. An added benefit of creating markers in Prelude is that the marker is stored with the clip and travels with it from one application to another, such as from Prelude to Premiere Pro.

You can apply markers from the Marker Type panel. However, it is much more efficient to apply markers using keyboard shortcuts. (This also allows you to apply markers in real time while watching playback.)

To apply a marker, type one of the following keyboard shortcuts. This places the marker, extends the duration to the end of the clip, and displays the marker HUD—the Heads-Up Display—where you can enter a title and a description.

Shortcut	Action
1	Sets start of Subclip marker
2	Sets start of Comment marker
3	Sets start of Flash Cue Point marker
4	Sets start of Web Link marker
5	Sets start of Chapter marker
6	Sets start of Speech Transcription marker
7 – 0	Sets start of Custom marker template

What's This HUD Thingy?

The HUD is a fast way to enter marker data

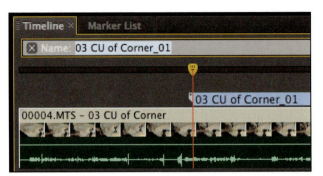

The Marker HUD (Heads-Up Display) appears when you create a new marker. It allows you to quickly enter the title, or description, of a marker without having to go to the Marker Inspector panel.

However, if you are entering markers during playback, the HUD seems to get in your way, because when you type "I" or "O" to create an In or Out for a marker, it actually types that as text.

What you need is the Option (or, um, an Alternative) to set durations.

Darn, you guessed! When the HUD is open, press **Option+I** to set the In, **Option+O** to set the Out. (Windows users use **Alt+I** or **Alt+O**, instead.)

In addition to Opt/Alt+I and Opt/Alt+O, Opt/Alt can be combined with J-K-L and H transport controls to control playback if necessary while typing into the HUD.

Create a Marker template

Templates speed logging clips in real time

A Marker Template is one of the existing six marker types that is saved with a Title and/or a Description and assigned to its own keyboard shortcut.

If you are always logging clips with the same marker, then adding the same title—such as "Good Take"—templates are designed for you.

To create a template, create a marker and give it a Title and Description. Then, go to **Marker > Save as Template**, and give the template a name. (You don't need to use the word "template" in the name.)

(Continued)

The first four Marker Templates that you create are assigned keyboard shortcuts **7**, **8**, **9**, or **0**. This means it is now very fast to apply a template to a clip while viewing the clip in real time. (Think of this as high-speed power logging!)

Customize the Marker List

Create your own list of markers, once you've created a template

Once a marker template is saved and added to the list of markers, the Marker Type panel can be further customized to remove markers that you no longer need. Right-click in the grey area to the right of a marker button to delete it or move it.

This is a handy tip to make sure only that the buttons you use are shown. However, you can't modify the list of markers until you have a custom marker button list, which is created when you modify and save a template.

Subclips Are the Heart of Prelude

Subclips allow you to log, select, and export portions of a clip

Subclips are markers that allow you to select portions of a clip. The sole reason for using subclips is to collect the best clips and parts of clips and send them over to either Premiere Pro or Final Cut Pro.

There is no limit to the number of subclips you have associated with a clip. Clips, as you can see from this screen shot, have blue rectangular icons. Subclips use a pair of In/Out marks. (The green dot means the clip is currently open in the Prelude Timeline.)

You can use whole clips, but, most of the time, subclips are better because you can select exactly the material you need within a clip.

(Continued)

The keyboard shortcut to set a Subclip is "1."

Note: Creating subclips does not create new media files. Subclips are simply pointers that point to a section of a larger clip. Adding subclips does not require more media storage.

Using Rough Cuts

A rough cut is a collection of selected clips and subclips

In spite of its name, a Rough Cut is not an edit; it's more like a collection of clips gathered into one spot for editing. Think of a Rough Cut as a "selects reel," not an edit.

You use Rough Cuts—and there's no limit to the number you can create—to select the clips and portions of clips you want to send to an editor. The editor, then, crafts them into a story.

Rough cuts contain collections of clips and subclips. They cannot contain any layers, transitions, or effects. They aren't an edit, they're a collection.

Adding Other Markers to a Rough Cut

Rough cuts can contain other marker types

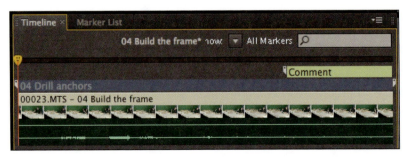

Rough cuts can contain more than clips and subclips. In fact, any marker can be added to a rough cut. Here's how ...

With a Rough Cut open, also open a source clip containing markers. Select the marker(s) you wish to add to the rough cut, either in the Timeline panel or in the Marker List panel then choose **Rough Cut > Add Selected Markers**.

Zooming on a Window

Maximizing or restoring frames

If you select a window and press the Tilde key (~) in the top left corner of your keyboard, it expands that window to full screen. (Adobe sometimes calls this key the "Accent" key.)

Press Tilde (~) again, and the window shrinks into its normal workspace.

Keyboard Shortcut System for Multiple Editors

Easily create custom keyboard shortcut sets

If you have multiple editors that are all using the same computer, each editor could create their own keyboard shortcuts and save them as a set.

To access the Keyboard Shortcut Utility, go up to the Prelude menu and click **Keyboard Shortcuts**. This opens the Keyboard Shortcut window. It is grouped in two broad categories: Keyboard Shortcuts within the Application, and Keyboard Shortcuts within Panels.

Each of the menus that appear at the top of Prelude has their own twirl-down option.

To change a keyboard shortcut, click the shortcut in the list that you want to change. Notice that it is highlighted. Then simply type the new keyboard shortcut.

To save this as a set of keyboard shortcuts, click the **Save As** button and give your shortcuts a name, then click **Save**. You can easily switch between the default shortcut set and your customized shortcut set.

Concatenate on Ingest

New feature allows selecting multiple clips and ingesting into a single clip

New with the 1.01 update is concatenation. What this does is allow you to group a variety of different clips into a single new clip during ingest. In order for concatenation to work, you must have both Adobe Media Encoder and Premiere Pro CS6 installed on your system.

To activate this, in the Ingest window, select all the clips you want to ingest, then, in the Transfer Options panel on the right, check the **Concatenate** check box and give the soon-to-be-combined files a name.

Click **OK**, and all the selected clips are combined in one file.

CAUTION! When concatenating clips, source clip timecode is reset to 00:00:00:00. Concatenation should be avoided if you need to reference the original timecode of the source media.

Cool Keyboard Shortcuts

Work faster using shortcuts

Prelude has dozens of keyboard shortcuts, but here are some of my favorites.

Ingest

Shortcut	What It Does
V	Ingest window: Checks selected items
Shift+V	Ingest Window: Checks all items
Control+Shift+V	Ingest window: Unchecks all items
I / O	Set In/Set Out

Logging

Shortcut	What It Does
H	Move playhead back five seconds
Alt/Option+H	Moves playhead back five seconds when the marker HUD is open
Shift+Left Arrow/Right Arrow	Jump playhead left/right five frames
[comma] / [period]	Move selected clip left/right one clip in Rough-cut
Control/Cmd+Left Arrow/Right Arrow	Jump to previous/next marker
1-6	Add one of six marker types at playhead
Shift-click	Selects multiple markers
Control/Command+N	Create new rough-cut
Shift+5	Display/Select Marker Inspector panel
Alt/Option+Left Arrow/Right Arrow	Select clip to left/right in rough-cut

CHAPTER 4

Premiere Pro—Preferences and Customization

We now shift our attention to Adobe Premiere Pro. The purpose of this chapter is to show you how to optimize your preferences, customize the interface, and put a lot of helpful keyboard shortcuts all in one place.

This is where we put all that technical stuff we learned in the first chapter to work. We'll start by learning how to reset the system back to square one.

Delete Preferences During Startup

Deleting preferences resets your system to factory defaults.

Sometimes, and it isn't your fault, Premiere starts acting weird. Most of the time, this is caused by corrupted preference settings. Premiere makes it easy to delete your preferences and return your system to a like-new state.

- If you are on a Mac, hold **Shift+Option** while launching Premiere from the Dock or Applications folder.

(*Continued*)

● If you are on Windows, hold **Shift+Alt** while launching Premiere from the Start-up bar or Applications folder.

You know you did this correctly when the Premiere Pro splash screen doesn't display the names of any past projects.

Deleting preferences does not affect any projects or media that you've worked on. However, it WILL reset any customized settings, like workspaces, that you've created, but not saved to disk.

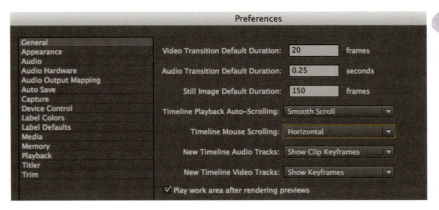

Optimizing General Preferences

Everyone is different, so, here's what i use

Preferences are exactly that—your preferences on how the program should work. But there are a number of preferences you should think about, so let me show you some of my favorite settings.

I prefer faster dissolves, so I set:

● Video Transition Default Duration to **20** frames (2/3's of a second at 29.97 fps)

● Audio Transition Default Duration to **0.25** seconds

Transition durations are fairly obvious. However, the Timeline will automatically scroll to keep the playhead (CTI) in view. If you have a fast computer, select **Smooth Scrolling** to smoothly slide the Timeline to the right during playback. If your computer is older, select **Page View**, to scroll right each time the playhead leaves the frame. So, my settings are:

● Timeline Playback to **Smooth Scrolling**

(Continued)

Scrolling the Timeline horizontally means that when you roll the scroll wheel on your mouse, the Timeline slides left or right. The other option is up and down (vertically). So, my settings are:

● Timeline Mouse Scrolling to **Horizontal**

Note: What's the CTI? Adobe used to call the thing that moves in the Timeline to show what's currently displayed in the Program monitor the "Current Time Indicator," or CTI. I was never comfortable with that, so I call it the playhead. In fact, Adobe replaced the term "CTI" with "playhead" starting with the CS5.5 release.

Any Color You Want ...

As long as it is some shade of gray

The basic rule of interfaces is that you don't want the brightness of the interface interfering with your ability to see the colors of your video.

Premiere Pro CS 5.5 set the background to 50 percent gray. CS 6.0 sets it somewhat darker. However, you can change this gray-scale value based on your particular needs, or the ambient lighting of your editing environment.

❶ Choose **Premiere Pro > Preferences > Appearance** (Mac OS) or **Edit > Preferences > Appearance** (Windows).

❷ Drag the slider to adjust the tonal value.

❸ Click **OK** when you are satisfied with the result.

Personally, I like darker interfaces because they make the colors in the video seem more vibrant.

[Auto] Save Your Work

Premiere pro automatically saves your work every twenty minutes

Saving your work every so often is an excellent idea ... especially when Premiere Pro does it for you. Auto-save backups are totally different versions of your project file. They are stored in a different place, using a different name.

The default settings save your work every twenty minutes and keep the five most recent Auto-saved copies. By default, Premiere Pro stores these files in the Premiere Pro Auto-Save folder, with other scratch disks.

Keep in mind that Premiere only creates an auto-save file when there are unsaved changes in a project. So, if you go to lunch and leave your project file open, Premiere will not be saving extra copies of that file while you are gone.

If you frequently make changes to a project, then wait a long time before saving, increase the number of retained versions in this preference.

For my work, I tend to save a bit more frequently—every ten to fifteen minutes— and keep fifteen to twenty of the most recent projects. Project files are tiny, when compared to media, so keeping a few extra versions doesn't take a whole lot of space.

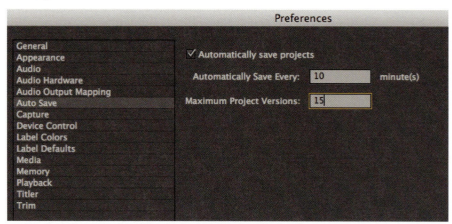

Set Media Preferences Carefully

Cache files help premiere work faster

The Media Preferences pane has a tremendous impact on overall system performance, because it controls where all your media work files will be stored.

Media Cache files and databases are work files and temporary files that Premiere uses during editing and when sharing media between applications. For best results, these should also be stored somewhere other than the boot disk. Specifically where you store them is up to you.

For example, here, I've created two separate folders on a separate drive from the boot disk:

● Premiere Media Cache

● Premiere Media Database

There is no magic to the folder name, but I like to keep the name obvious so I know what the folder is used for. Click the **Browse** button to navigate to and select the appropriate folder.

I also generally recommend storing cache files separately from media.

Clean Up Your Cache

Cleaning the cache can fix problems and speed workflow

As we've discussed, Premiere Pro creates a variety of work files to assist in displaying audio waveforms, thumbnails, and displaying media. These work files are stored in the Media Cache folder and tracked in the Media Cache Database. The Media Database also allows Premiere to share media with other Adobe applications without having to recreate these work files, which speeds data interchange between the apps.

Most of the time, once you have these preferences set, you don't need to worry about them. However, if performance ever becomes sluggish, or files are not displayed properly, cleaning these cache files may become necessary. To do so, go to: **Preferences > Media** and click the **Clean** button next to Media Databases.

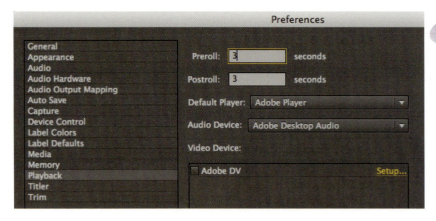

Faster Previews

In this case, it's okay to "play around"

There is a very cool edit preview shortcut—**Shift + K**—that plays around the current position of the playhead. What this does is move the playhead back two seconds, play through the edit point, stop two seconds after the edit point, and reset the playhead back to its original position. Adobe calls this "Play Around."

(Continued)

All with one shortcut! I use this constantly, except I don't like the two-second duration. So, in Preferences > Playback, I change the Preroll and Postroll each to three seconds.

The slightly longer duration helps me to get into the flow of the edit.

Workspaces Are Cool

Change the window layout by switching workspaces

Workspaces are collections of frames and panels assembled into a consistent interface. Workspaces help you work faster by putting all the essential tools for a particular function—such as editing—all in one layout.

Workspaces are composed of frames which contain panels which contain specific settings or functions—such as the Viewer and Program monitors, Timecode display, or Timeline. Panels are labeled by tabs, but I will refer to them principally as panels.

Premiere Pro has six prebuilt preferences, which you select from either the Workspace popup menu in the top right corner of the screen, or by choosing **Window > Workspace**.

You can change workspaces at any time with no damage to your project. You're just moving the furniture here, not tearing down the house.

Note: The CS6 version of Premiere Pro has a significantly different interface compared to the CS5.5 version. Because many longtime Premiere editors may not be comfortable with all the changes, Adobe included a CS5.5 workspace, which is also available from the Workspace menu.

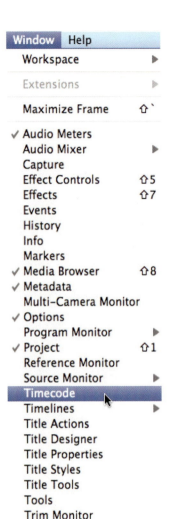

Repanel the House

Any panel in any frame can be moved or removed

The Window menu lists twenty-seven different panels (panels are labeled with tabs at the top of a frame) that can be added, moved, or removed from any workspace. However, not all of them are displayed at once. In fact, most of them are not.

You can see which ones are displayed by selecting the **Window** menu. Tabs that are displayed in the current workspace have a checkmark. Those that aren't, don't.

To open a tab in its own window, select it from the **Window** menu.

Move a Panel

Watch the purple shapes to position a tab into a workspace

To move a panel and dock it into a frame, grab the tab in the gripper area (on the left side of the tab) and drag it. As you move it across the interface, one of five different purple shapes appears. These purple shapes are called "docking zones."

For instance, here, the purple shape is at the top of the panel. Release the mouse and the tab appears above the other tabs in that panel.

Here are the five different positions for positioning a tab:

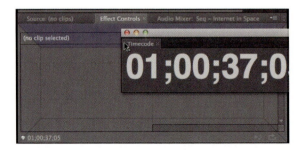

(Continued)

Location of Purple Docking Zone	What Happens
Center of panel	The Panel tab appears at top of panel, with other tabs.
Left edge of panel	The Panel tab appears in its own panel to left of the selected panel.
Top edge of panel	The Panel tab appears in its own panel above the selected panel.
Right edge of panel	The Panel tab appears in its own panel to right of the selected panel.
Bottom edge of panel	The Panel tab appears in its own panel below the selected panel.

Create a Floating Panel

Undock a tab to create a floating panel in its own window

In the top right corner of each panel are four small horizontal lines; Adobe calls this the "Panel menu." Click this icon and select **Undock Panel** from the menu to turn the selected panel (the one surrounded with a gold edge) into a floating panel contained in its own window.

For example, if you have a dual-monitor computer system, this makes it easy to drag a panel from one monitor to another.

Select **Undock Frame** to turn all the panels in that frame into a single floating window.

Once you've undocked a Frame, you can't redock it by using Undo. The easiest way to restore things is to reset the workspace, which I'll explain in a minute.

Remove a Tab

"X" marks the spot …

It isn't very big, but see that small "x" to the right of the panel's name in the tab? That's the Remove button.

Click it and, poof!, no more tab. Gone. History. Toast.

(Continued)

Nope, Undo won't bring it back. However, don't despair, all is not lost. Go back to the Window menu and select it. Then, drag it back into your workspace wherever you want.

A Fast—and Faster—Way to Enlarge a Panel

Too cool for school

Here's a fast way to expand any selected panel to full screen. (By the way, a panel is selected when there's a gold box around it.)

Select a panel and type **Shift+`** (that's the key in the top left corner of your keyboard just underneath the ESC key). Type **Shift+`** to reset it back to normal.

Yawn. This is, I'm sure, both simple and useful. BUT, an even cooler trick is to roll your mouse over a panel and press **`** (that accent key in the upper left corner of your keyboard again). This expands whatever window the mouse is hovering in up to full screen. You don't even have to select it first!

This is a *REALLY* fast way to enlarge any window, like the Media Browser or Project panel, to full screen so you can actually see what you are doing.

Wow!

Note: Here's a hidden shortcut. To enlarge either the Source or Program monitors to full-screen, with no interface elements, select the monitor, then press **Ctrl+`** (Mac or Windows). Instant movies! (Type it again to return to normal.)

Customize Your Workspaces

Customizing workspaces allows a great deal of flexibility

I love customizing my workspace! For example, drag any horizontal or vertical black line between two frames to change their size. Or, remove panels you don't want. Add panels you do. Go crazy!

(Continued)

Then, when you've changed everything to your satisfaction, select **Window > Workspace > New Workspace**.

This saves your interface wizardry for reuse whenever you need it.

Note: Even if you don't save the workspace, Premiere remembers the current workspace layout when you save your project or quit Premiere. This means if you only need a workspace for a short while, you don't need to save it. (In fact, the workspace travels with the project, so if you open it on a different computer, you'll still see the same workspace.)

Reset a Workspace

For those rare instances when you've screwed up beyond all repair

What? Oh, you've managed to make a complete mess of reorganizing your workspace. Worse, every time you quit Premiere and reopen it, you are haunted by workspace errors from times past.

Not to panic. There's hope.

Go to **Window > Workspace > Reset workspace**. Premiere asks if you want to reset everything back to normal—or the last time you saved a custom workspace.

Click "**Yes**," and all is reset back to normal.

Audio	⌥⇧1
Color Correction	⌥⇧2
• Editing	⌥⇧3
Editing (CS5.5)	⌥⇧4
Effects	⌥⇧5
Larry's Incredible Workspace	⌥⇧6
Metalogging	⌥⇧7
New Workspace...	
Delete Workspace...	
Reset Current Workspace...	
✓ Import Workspace from Projects	

Delete a Workspace

For those times when giving up is the best option

If you no longer need a custom workspace, choose **Window > Workspace > Delete Workspace**. Premiere asks if you want to delete the current workspace. Say "Yes," and it's gone.

While you cannot delete any Adobe-supplied workspaces, you can delete any custom workspaces that you, or someone using your name, created. *(Continued)*

89

Undo does not bring back a deleted workspace.

Create a Project Template

A fast way to create a custom project you can reuse

Thinking of customizing your environment, you can create project templates for Premiere. If you frequently work with the same style of project, consider making a template or starter project.

Either create a new project or take an existing project and save a copy using **File > Save As**.

Inside the project, organize your bins for graphics, sound effects, titles, music, and so on. If you wish, create subsequences for the title sequence, show bumpers, and closing segments. Close and save the project file.

At the Finder or Explorer level, locate the project file.

Show the item properties by right-clicking on the file icon.

Lock the project file by checking the "Lock" checkbox.

In the future, simply launch the project. By locking the file, the project opens as an untitled, new project, but with all your customization intact.

Simply use **File > Save As** to save the project with a new name and you are good to go.

The Wrench Icon

This icon reveals a menu with access to scopes and other displays

The wrench icon (Adobe calls it the "Settings menu," which is far less sexy) in the lower right corner of the Source and Program monitors provides access to

(Continued)

a host of display options. These include all the video scopes, closed captioning, dropped frame indicators, and a variety of other controls that are turned off by default in order to reduce clutter on both monitor displays.

This is clearly a case where throwing a wrench in the works is a good thing.

Psst! Hey, Wanna Buy a Button?

Customize the buttons in both source and program panels

One of the big new interface changes in Premiere CS6 is the slimmed down interface. A lot of the clutter and excess buttons are gone. This is a great thing, unless your favorite button was one of those that got whacked.

Never fear, though, there's a cool way to get them back: the Button Editor. In the lower right corner of both the Source and Program panels (just below the monitors) is a plus (+) icon. Click it to reveal the Button Editor, which allows you to customize your interface.

Personally, I love having one-click access to Safe Zones, so I use the Button Editor to add that button to my display.

However, though I do a lot of customization on my own system, for this book I'm working with all the standard workspaces as shipped by Adobe to keep screen shots from getting too confusing.

Shortcuts! Get Your Shortcuts HERE!!

Use what you know and retain muscle memory

Adobe Premiere Pro CS6 has four families of keyboard shortcuts:

- Premiere Pro CS 6.0

- Premiere Pro CS 5.5

- Avid Media Composer 5

- Final Cut Pro 7.0

What's really nice about being able to select from different shortcut groups is that if you are migrating to Premiere from another editor, you don't need to teach your fingers new tricks. Simply select the shortcut set that fits what you know and let your fingers go back to work

You can change your shortcuts at any time. Go to **Premiere Pro > Keyboard Shortcuts** (Mac OS) or **Edit > Keyboard Shortcuts** (Windows).

Customize Your Keyboard Shortcuts

Make premiere pro work the way you want to work

Not only can you select entire keyboard shortcut sets, or collections of shortcuts, you can customize any shortcut.

1 In the Mac OS and CS6, choose **Premier Pro > Keyboard Shortcuts** (In Windows and Premiere Pro CS5.5 and earlier, choose **Edit > Keyboard Customization**).

2 To create a single, new shortcut, scroll or search for the menu item to which you want to apply the shortcut until it appears in the Command column.

(Continued)

❸ If necessary, click the triangle next to the name of a category to reveal the commands it includes. Commands are grouped by menu and, if necessary, submenu. (You can only add shortcuts to specific menu commands, not menu groups.)

❹ Double-click in the Shortcut field to select the shortcut and open it for editing.

❺ Type the shortcut you want to use for the item. The Keyboard Customization dialog box displays an alert if the shortcut you choose is already in use.

❻ Now, you have several choices:

- Click **Undo** to erase a shortcut and return it to the original command setting.

- If there's a conflict between shortcuts, click **Go To** to jump to the command that previously had the shortcut.

- Click **Clear** to simply delete the shortcut you typed

- Click **Redo** to undo the shortcut you just cleared.

See? All kinds of options. Then, repeat this process to enter as many shortcuts as you want. When you're finished, click **Save As**, type a name for your Key Set, and click **Save**.

Note: Final Cut users, note that Premiere Pro CS6 does not have "double-tap" keyboard shortcuts. In FCP, we would type R+R to select the Ripple tool. In Premiere, we can't do that. We need to create a separate shortcut.

Setting Up Dual Monitors

Running two computer monitors at once gives you a whole lot more room to see

Premiere Pro can drive two, or more, computer monitors which allows you to see much more of the interface, or more of your image.

You have two choices: using an AJA, Blackmagic Design, or Matrox interface to connect a video monitor to your system. This provides a dedicated video monitor which can be calibrated for precise color work, as well as the ability to capture from, or output to, a wide variety of video tape decks. All three of these companies support Thunderbolt, which allows their gear to connect to Macs that don't support adding interface cards.

Or, you can add a second graphics card to your system—for those computer systems that support adding additional graphics cards—and connect a second computer monitor. This allows you to display interface elements, such as Safe Margins and transport controls on your second computer display.

Use the operating system Control Panel to determine monitor placement. Then, in Premiere go to the **Preferences > General** tab to configure the monitors.

Note: To make sure your monitor displays colors accurately and consistently, consider purchasing a Spyder4Pro monitor calibration tool (spyder.datacolor.com).

Setting Preferences for Indeterminate Media

Indeterminate media means stills and other nonanimated images

Indeterminant media is a fancy word for still image, or any other file that doesn't have a definite duration; the duration is "indeterminant."

In **Premiere Pro > Preferences > Media** (**Edit > Preferences > Media** in Windows) you can specify the timebase of all imported still images,

(*Continued*)

whether timecode for each clips starts at 00:00:00:00 or at the timecode associated with the imported media (still images don't have timecode, so 00:00:00:00 is the best choice here) and whether the frame count starts at 0 or 1.

My recommendation is to set the timebase to match your sequence, set the timecode to start at 00:00:00:00, and set the frame count to start at 1.

Setting Preferences for Growing Files

The game isn't over, but you still gotta edit!

A Growing File is a file that has not finished transferring. A classic example is capturing the video from a sports contest. You need to start editing highlights before the game is complete. So, you capture the sports video as a growing file, which Premiere allows you to edit while the capture is ongoing.

Not all video formats support growing files. QuickTime, for instance, does not. However, OP1A MXF does, which is why broadcasters depend upon this format.

The growing files preference setting (in the Media section) allows you to import files that are not yet complete and have Premiere automatically refresh the Project panel and the files in it as new material is added to it. If you decide to automatically refresh these files, you can also determine how frequently this update should occur.

My recommendation is that if growing files are new to you, leave the default settings alone. As you get more experience, you can tweak to suit.

Keyboard Shortcuts for Tools

Sorted alphabetically to simplify your life

As part of our continuing effort to make your life simpler and faster, here is a list of all the tools, sorted in alphabetical order (according to the Premiere Pro CS6 shortcut set).

Never let it be said that we don't go the extra mile around here.

Tool	Windows and Mac OS
Hand tool	H
Pen tool	P
Rate Stretch tool	X
Razor tool	C
Ripple Edit tool	B
Rolling Edit tool	N
Selection tool	V
Slide tool	U
Slip tool	Y
Track Select tool	A
Zoom tool	Z

More Useful Keyboard Shortcuts

A grab bag of handy tricks

All these are based on the Premiere Pro CS6 keyboard shortcut set.

Task	Windows	Mac OS
Fit entire sequence in Timeline	\	\
Zoom into Timeline	+	+
Zoom out of Timeline	-	-
Select Project panel	Shift+1	Shift+1
Select Source monitor	Shift+2	Shift+2
Select Timeline	Shift+3	Shift+3
Select Program monitor	Shift+4	Shift+4
Select Media Browser	Shift+8	Shift+8
Display Audio Workspace	Shift+Alt+1	Shift+Option+1
Display Color Correction Workspace	Shift+Alt+2	Shift+Option+2
Display Editing Workspace	Shift+Alt+3	Shift+Option+3
Display Effects Workspace	Shift+Alt+5	Shift+Option+5
Display Metalogging Workspace	Shift+Alt+6	Shift+Option+6

(Continued)

Cool Titler Keyboard Shortcuts

Simple shortcuts for faster ttitles

Here are some keyboard shortcuts that make creating titles a lot easier. Sure, anybody can move text, but can you create the registered trademark symbol with a single shortcut?

And I love the ability to position text next to a title safe margin. (This shortcut only works in the Titler, not in the Program Monitor.)

Check these out!

Result	Windows	Mac OS
Create New title	Ctrl+T	Command+T
Insert bullet		Option+8
Insert copyright symbol	Ctrl+Alt+Shift+C	Option+C
Insert registered trademark symbol	Ctrl+Alt+Shift+R	Option+R
Insert trademark symbol		Option+2
Insert degree symbol		Shift+Option+8
Nudge selected object 5 pixels down	Shift+Down Arrow	Shift+Down Arrow
Nudge selected object 1 pixel down	Down Arrow	Down Arrow
Nudge selected object 5 pixels to the left	Shift+Left Arrow	Shift+Left Arrow
Nudge selected object 1 pixel to the left	Left Arrow	Left Arrow
Nudge selected object 5 pixels to the right	Shift+Right Arrow	Shift+Right Arrow
Nudge selected object 1 pixel to the right	Right Arrow	Right Arrow
Nudge selected object 5 pixels up	Shift+Up Arrow	Shift+Up Arrow
Nudge selected object 1 pixel up	Up Arrow	Up Arrow
Position objects to the bottom title-safe margin	Ctrl+Shift+D	Command+Shift+D
Position objects to the left title-safe margin	Ctrl+Shift+F	Command+Shift+F
Position objects to the top title-safe margin	Ctrl+Shift+O	Command+Shift+O

CHAPTER 5

Premiere Pro—Navigation and Interface

Now that we have Premiere Pro setup and ready to fly, let's check into some ways we can optimize the interface, navigate faster, and, in general, bend this system to our will.

A Purple Wedge is Not a Bad Thing

Purple is the color to watch when customizing the interface

We touched on this in an earlier chapter, but the ability to drag tabs and move them into different places on the interface is a huge benefit.

For example, I move the Timecode window down next to the Audio Meters so that I have a nice big set of numbers telling me exactly where I am at all times. To place the timecode to the left of the Audio Meters, select **Window > Timecode** to open the tab in a floating window.

Then, drag the tab down until the wedge (called the "Docking Zone") on the left side of the Audio Meters lights up. When you let go of the mouse, the timecode window is placed to the left of the Audio Meters.

(Continued)

(Thinking about the Audio Meters, check out Chapter 7 for a whole flock of tips on working with audio and the Audio Meters inside Premiere Pro.)

The Secrets of the Mouse

No, that isn't the title to the latest independent film

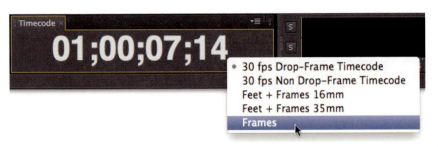

The entire Premiere Pro interface is loaded with hundreds of hidden shortcuts—all available at the click of a mouse—a *right*-click, that is.

The cool thing about these contextual menus is that they change depending upon where you click. The benefit to using these, instead of keyboard shortcuts, is that you don't have to take your hands off the mouse to use them.

And anything that saves time is a good thing in my book.

Note: The reason that I used the Panel menu from the TIMECODE panel was that, at five lines, I could fit it into the screen shot. Most of these menus have dozens of really helpful choices.

A Faster Way to Configure a Sequence

Finally! configure a sequence without understanding codecs!

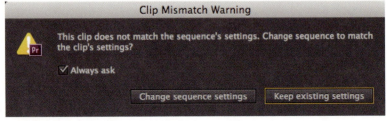

One of the big challenges for most video editors is figuring out how to match the sequence settings to the video format. Sometimes, this can be really, really difficult because you needed to know all the technical specifications of the video to properly configure the sequence for editing.

(Continued)

Starting with the CS5 release, Adobe simplified this by auto-configuring the sequence when you dragged a video clip on top of the **New Item** button in the Project panel. However, that step wasn't necessarily intuitive.

Adobe made this much easier with the CS6 release. Simply *drag* or edit a clip into an empty sequence and, if the settings don't match, Premiere pops up a dialog asking if you want to change the sequence settings to match the clip, or render the clip to match the sequence settings.

Much, much easier. Yay!!

Note: This configuration dialog only appears when you drag a clip into an empty sequence. Editing a clip using keyboard shortcuts, or the Overwrite/Insert buttons will leave the sequence settings intact. Once a sequence contains a clip, its settings cannot be changed.

Hover Scrub Turn-Off

Toggle hover scrub on or off ... fast!

Hover Scrub is a hot new feature in CS6 that allows you to float your mouse over a clip and see what the clip looks like. This works wherever you view clips.

You turn Hover Scrub on, or off, by typing **Shift+H**.

What you may not know, however, is that you can also use a Panel menu from either the Project panel or the Media Browser panel to toggle hover scrub on or off.

Even better is that if hover scrub is turned off, you can temporarily turn it on by pressing the **Shift** key. As soon as you let go of the Shift key, hovering is turned off again.

Storyboard Your Images

Organize your images using a storyboard layout

Instead of looking at file names, you can organize your images using the icon view in the Project panel. This emulates a storyboard layout. A storyboard

(Continued)

layout allows you to quickly organize your images based on how they look, rather than file names.

Select the Project panel, then press the Accent key (top left corner of the keyboard under the ESC key) to zoom the window full-screen. This gives you some room to work.

Note: You could also use **Undock Panel** from the Panel menu in the Project panel. This turns the Project panel into a free-floating window. While it may be simpler to use Maximize, when you have a dual-monitor setup, floating the panel provides more flexibility.

Click the **Icon View** button in the extreme lower left corner of the Project window.

Drag clips in the panel to arrange them in the order you want to edit. Put the starting shot in the upper left corner, then flow shots from the top left to lower right.

If you want to view a clip, select it in the Project panel and press the **J**, **K**, or **L** keys to play the clip. With the clip selected, press **I** to set an In or **O** to set an Out. You no longer need to open a clip in the Source monitor to view or mark it.

Select the range of clips you want to edit into the Timeline by either **Shift-clicking**, or **Command-clicking** (Mac OS) or **Control-clicking** (Windows) to select any combination of clips.

Click the **Automate to Sequence** button in the low right corner of the Project panel (I'll cover this in another tip).

Poof! Instant edit.

Note: The **Automate to Sequence** button is inactive until one or more clips are selected.

Sort Your Thumbnails

Here's a cool way to organize your thumbnails

This tip was suggested by **Peter Tours**.

Maybe this is too obvious, but since you can't sort thumbnails by name or duration in the Project panel or bin, you can get around this with a simple technique.

Switch the thumbnails to List View, sort the text by name, duration, or any other Project panel column heding, select and copy all the clips, paste them into a new bin, change back to Icon View and voilá! Sorted thumbnails.

Secrets of the J-K-L Keys

Speed at your fingertips

When you really want to be a power junky, especially when you need to control a tape deck, nothing beats the J-K-L keys.

Just to refer to the basics:

- Type J once to play backwards at 1x speed.
- Type L once to play forwards at 1x speed.
- Type K to stop.

But you didn't buy this book just for the obvious stuff; you want to know the *devious* stuff as well.

- So, tap **J** or **L** multiple times. Each time you tap, speed increases by 1X up to 4X
- **Shift+J**—starts in slow motion, then gradually speeds up going in reverse.
- Press and hold **J+K**—play in slow motion reverse

(Continued)

- **Shift+L**—starts in slow motion, then gradually speeds up going forward.

- Press and hold **K+L**—slow motion forward

Variable Speed Changes

This is very cool—weird, but cool!

When you use the **J—K—L** keys to change clip playback speed in the Source or Program Monitor, you are speeding up the clip in discreet steps. If you want to change the speed of a clip variably, try this.

When a clip is playing, press and hold **Shift+L** to speed it up, or press and hold **Shift+J** to slow it down.

When a clip is stopped, press and hold **Shift+L** to ramp from slow-motion to fast forward. Press and hold **Shift+J** to ramp from slow-motion to fast reverse.

Play with this and you'll see what I mean. This works when a clip is playing forward or backward, fast or slow. Type these enough and the clip will change playback direction.

Try it.

Note: This is not the same as changing the speed of a clip in the Timeline. This simply affects the current playback speed. When you stop playback, the speed resets to normal.

Editing Offline Clips

Even if a clip is offline, you can still work with it

Normally, you'd think that if a clip is offline, you can't do anything with it. But Premiere Pro allows you to add information to your clip, even when it is offline.

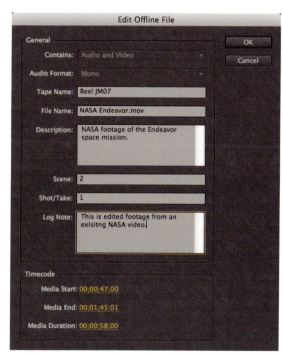

(Continued)

107

To open the dialog in this screen shot, double-click the clip icon in either Storyboard or List view. Then, add information into this dialog.

If you are capturing from tape, adding a Tape Name greatly simplifies the process of capturing—or, more important, recapturing—media from tape.

Reuse Your Sequences

Here's a fast way to import a sequence from one project into another

Wham! You just realized you need to import a sequence from last week's Project into this week's Project. Except ... how?

Not a problem! Importing sequences and projects isn't exactly obvious, but you can do it.

Here's how to do this in Premiere CS5.5:

❶ Open the Project you want to import the sequence, or Project, into.

❷ Go to **File > Import > Select Project**

❸ Choose either the entire Project, or select just a certain sequence.

❹ Make your choices and click **OK**.

In CS6, this changed a bit:

❺ Open the Project you want to import the sequence, or Project, into.

❻ Go to **File > Import**

❼ Select the Project that contains the sequences you want to import.

❽ In the dialog, specify whether you want to import the entire Project or just sequences.

❾ If you choose to import sequences, a second dialog appears allowing you to select which sequences you want to import.

(Continued)

10 Make your choices and click **OK**.

11 Premiere creates a new bin and stores the selected project, or sequences, inside.

Back It Up!

Duplicate your sequence before making major changes

It never fails.

The client *insists* you make changes to their latest edit. You work feverishly making the new cut and show it off proudly, only to have them tell you they want to go back to the original version. Except ... you don't have the original version any more.

You only need to experience that sinking feeling once to get in the habit of duplicating a working sequence before making major changes. The nice thing is that Premiere makes this fast and easy.

Select the sequence in the Project panel and select **Edit > Duplicate**, or right-click the Sequence name and select **Duplicate**.

Here are some naming conventions that have worked for many editors:

● If you have multiple editors working on the same project, make a backup copy and add your initials to the end of the sequence name.

● When making a daily backup, add the date at the end.

● If you are making a lot of changes to a sequence and want to play it safe, you can break it down even further by appending the time of day, for example, Music Video Rough Cut_121006_ Afternoon.

By getting into the habit of naming and backing up your sequences with a date, you'll save a lot of frustration in finding exactly the sequence you need.

(Continued)

Note: It is axiomatic in editing that any sequence labeled **Final** isn't.

Prevent Accidents: Lock It Down

Avoid accidental edits and deletions by locking a track

Have you ever had that sinking feeling that you just destroyed an edit because you deleted something that shouldn't have been deleted? Yup, me too.

You can minimize the fear factor by locking your tracks. Here's how:

- Click the **Toggle Track Lock** icon—that small blank square in the track header—to lock an individual audio or video track.

- Shift+click a **Toggle Track Lock** button to lock ALL audio or video tracks at the same time.

- To work on one track and lock all others, Shift+click the **Toggle Track Lock** to lock all tracks, then click the **Toggle Track Lock** for a single track to unlock just the track you want to work on.

You can't apply passwords to lock, or unlock, a track. When a track is locked, diagonal hash lines appear in the track.

Use Project Manager to Consolidate Media

Project manager provides media cleanup and consolidation

The Project Manager allows you to manage and consolidate media. Use Project Manager if you need to bundle the media of a project into a single location, or remove unwanted footage. It can archive or consolidate a project based upon a selection or a sequence.

1 In the Project panel, select a sequence or bin. You can hold down the **Command** (Mac OS) or **Control** (Windows) key to select multiple items.

(Continued)

Choose **Project > Project Manager**. The Project Manager window opens.

3 In the Project Manager window, confirm that you have selected the desired sources by looking at the top of the window. The Resulting Project section offers two options:

(a) **Create New Trimmed Project**, creates a new project based on other options in the window and references the original media

(b) **Collect Files and Copy to New Location**, gathers media and copies it to a new location of your choice

4 Depending on which option you choose in the Resulting Project section, you'll have different options available to process the media. These include excluding unused clips, making an offline version of the project, adding handles, including conform files, and renaming the actual media files to match clip names.

5 Specify where you want to save the files using the **Project Destination** settings.

6 Click **OK** to finish.

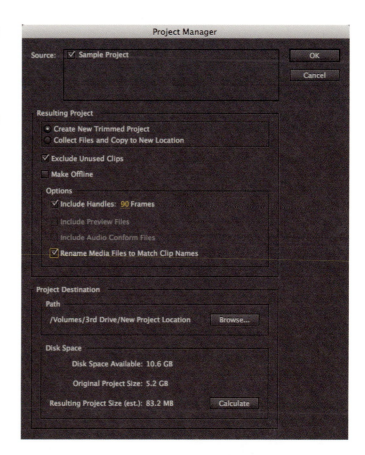

Project Manager—Advanced Tips

Some additional thoughts to help manage media

To improve speed when copying files, I always try to store media on a different hard disk than its current location.

To provide more flexibility when editing, I try to set handles longer than the default 30 frames. I prefer 90 to 100.

I tend to use Project Manager only when a project is complete. When I am in the middle of a complex project, I prefer to leave everything alone, unless I'm having problems.

Note: The Project manager does not gather dynamic-linked elements and it is not able to trim every video format to remove unused media. For instance, RED R3D files can only be moved or collected as whole clips. This is a really good reason to capture media in shorter chunks.

Zoom Smart

One fast way to see the big picture

You've got your head buried in the details of your edit, but you need to take a quick look at the big picture of the entire Timeline. The problem is pressing **Plus** or **Minus** takes forever, you'll lose your train of thought.

Zoom to Sequence to the rescue!

Use Zoom to Sequence in the Timeline to switch between detailed and global views of your sequence with one key press. Press to zoom the timeline to show the entire contents of your sequence. Press again to return to the previous zoom level.

What's the secret key? \

Put a Marker in a Clip

Add markers to clips in the source monitor

You can add markers to a clip, but you can't do it in the Timeline.

Open a clip in the source monitor and position the playhead where you want the marker to appear.

(Continued)

Type **M**.

Type **M** a second time to open the Marker dialog box, where you can add titles, comments, or change the type of marker. (You can also open a marker for editing by double-clicking the marker itself.)

When you edit the clip into the Timeline, the clip markers will travel with it. However, if you need to modify or remove a clip marker, you'll need to open the clip back in the source monitor to do so.

Markers Have Options

The marker dialog box has expanded your choices

When you double-click a marker to edit it, whether in the source monitor or the Timeline, the Marker dialog appears. This allows you to refine the marker location, change its duration, and alter the title and comments.

However, you can also switch the marker from a standard Comment marker to either a Chapter Marker (which works in Encore, DVD Studio Pro, or compressed H.264 files for the web), or a Web Link (which works in QuickTime).

You can also embed Flash Cue Points, to trigger a Flash action when playback reaches that particular point in your movie.

Note: While markers are fully supported within the Premiere Pro Timeline, not all video file formats support all these different marker types when they are exported.

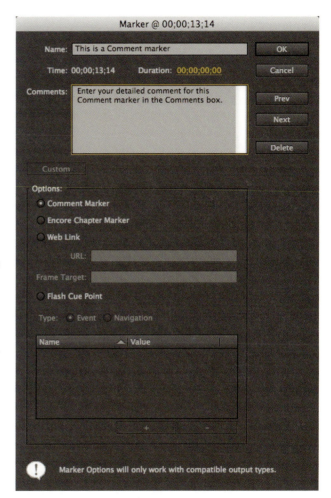

New Keyboard Shortcuts for Markers

Marker shortcuts changed in CS6

With the CS6 release of Premiere Pro, the keyboard shortcuts to create and navigate to markers have changed. Here are the new settings:

Task	Mac	Windows
Add Marker	M	M
Go to Next Marker	Shift+M	Shift+M
Go to Previous Marker	Shift+Command+M	Shift+Control+M
Delete Current Marker	Option+M	Alt+M
Delete All Markers	Option+Command+M	Alt+Control+M

More Marker Secrets

The hidden ways of markers

In addition to keyboard shortcuts, the Marker panel is a fast way to see, and jump to, all your markers.

To display all markers associated with a clip or a sequence, select the clip or sequence, then choose **Window > Markers**.

To jump to ANY marker, click the marker name in the Markers panel.

To modify a marker, double-click the marker name in the Markers panel.

To delete a marker, double-click a marker to open the Marker dialog, then click the **Delete** button.

Deciding When to Render

The colors are the clues

Most of the time, Premiere Pro can play back your sequence in real-time with high-quality, full frame-rate images by harnessing the power of the Mercury Playback Engine. However, every so often, you'll create an effect that is so complex, it needs to render for optimum playback.

How can you tell if rendering is necessary? By the color of the render bar at the top of the Timeline.

Render bar color	What it means
Red	An unrendered section that needs to be rendered to play back the sequence in real time and at full frame rate.
Yellow	An unrendered section that is complex, but may not need to be rendered in order to play back the sequence in real time and at full frame rate.
Green	A section that has already been rendered.

Note: What does render mean? It's a weird word with a simple meaning. To "render" means to "calculate." To render an effect means we are calculating the effect and turning it into video, or audio.

Faster Ways to Render

The work area controls what renders and what doesn't

The only problem with rendering is that it takes time. Sometimes a lot of time. Even a LONG time! Worse, Premiere wants to render the entire sequence, when all you really need to render is just a small portion.

That's where the work area can help. This is a gray bar that spans the entire duration of the sequence. It has a small gold "bumper" on each end.

(Continued)

115

Grab the end of the gray bar and drag it where you want to start and stop rendering. Move the work area horizontally by dragging the small box in the middle of the gray bar.

Now, when you render, only the area under the work area will render. This trick, alone, can save you hours of time on each project!

Keyboard Shortcuts for the Work Area

Anything that saves me time is a good thing

Here are several keyboard shortcuts that can speed rendering:

Shortcut	Mac OS	Windows
Trim work area start to playhead position	Option+[	Atl+[
Trim work area end to playhead position	Option+]	Alt+]
Render all effects in work area	Return	Return

There are several other render options; however, they don't have keyboard shortcuts. They can be found in the Sequence menu.

Option has Options

(Or) the alternatives of Alt

If you hold the **Option** (Mac OS) or **Alt** (Windows) key when dragging a clip in the Timeline, Premiere CS6 will duplicate it.

If you click one side of a synced clip, say just the video or just the audio, while holding the **Option** (**Alt**) key, you can select just the portion of the clip you click. Then, you could trim or move just that portion of the clip.

(Continued)

Note: If you have already selected the entire clip, deselect it before **Option** (**Alt**)-clicking a clip. You can't select a portion of an already selected clip.

Nudging Clips in the Timeline

The keyboard shortcuts to nudge clips in the timeline have changed

With the CS6 release of Premiere Pro, the keyboard shortcuts to nudge clips have changed. This works with one or more selected clips; however, the clips must have room to move on the Timeline and can't be blocked by other clips on the same track.

Here are the new shortcuts:

Task	Mac	Windows
Nudge selected clip 1 frame right	Command+Right arrow	Alt+Right arrow
Nudge selected clip 5 frames right	Shift+Command+Right arrow	Shift+Alt+Right arrow
Nudge selected clip 1 frame left	Command+Left arrow	Alt+Left arrow
Nudge selected clip 5 frames left	Shift+Command+Left arrow	Shift+Alt+Left arrow

Note: You can change the number of frames a clip moves when you press the Shift key from the default setting of 5, by going to **Premiere Pro > Preferences > Trim** and changing the Large Trim Offset.

Set Your Timecode Free

New floating timecode panel easily displays timecode

CS6 added a new Timecode panel that makes viewing timecode—even from a great distance—a whole lot easier.

Open it using **Window > Timecode**.

(Continued)

Drag this to a second monitor, or dock it as part of your workspace. Right-click on it to select from a variety of display options.

Is Timecode time-of-day?

No, but it can be

Timecode is simply a label that uniquely identifies each frame of video. (Think of it as similar to the address of a house.) Because timecode expresses these addresses as locations in time, it is easy for software to calculate durations between any two points in the same clip or sequence.

If you aren't used to reading timecode, it expresses time using pairs of numbers: Hours:Minutes:Seconds:Frames. There is no necessary relationship between timecode and time of day. There can be, but it isn't required.

Note: For those that need to worry about whether timecode is drop-frame or non-drop-frame, check the punctuation between the last two pairs of numbers. Non-drop-frame timecode uses a colon (:) and drop-frame timecode uses a semi-colon (;). Most, but sadly not all, HD formats use non-drop-frame timecode.

The choice of using non-drop or drop-frame timecode is based almost exclusively on the camera native video format. Premiere automatically supports both formats.

Non-drop timecode is most often used for films and shorter projects, like commercials or trailers. Drop-frame timecode is often used for longer projects where the duration displayed in timecode needs to match the duration of the program in real time, such as television programs which must run to an exact length.

Note: In spite of its name, no frames are lost using "drop-frame" timecode. The difference is in how frames are numbered. The actual number of frames contained in a program are identical, regardless of which timecode numbering system you use.

Change Sequence Starting Timecode

This is a fast way to alter the starting time of your sequence

By default, the starting timecode for a sequence is 00:00:00:00, which works for most situations.

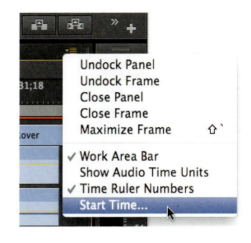

However, there are times when you need to change the starting timecode. To do this, click the panel menu in the top right corner of the Timeline and select **Start Time**. This opens a small dialog allowing you to change the starting timecode of your sequence.

Note: In North America, it is traditional for all programs to start at 01:00:00:00. In Europe, many programs start at 10:00:00:00. Unless you are told to use a certain starting timecode, the timecode you use for your project doesn't make any difference.

Watch Those Gestures

Premiere now supports Mac gestures

If you have a Mac trackpad, or Magic Mouse with a built-in trackpad, Premiere now responds to pinch gestures to zoom in or out.

Dragging two fingers horizontally scrolls across the Timeline. Dragging two fingers vertically scrolls up or down in the Timeline.

Throw a Wrench in Your Works

This lowly wrench makes a big difference in your display

It is easy to overlook, but this small wrench icon, called the Settings menu, located in both the Source and Program monitors, plays a big role in how your images are presented.

(Continued)

119

From its pop-up menu, you can display safe zones, interlace fields, video scopes, and a wide variety of other technical information. Don't let its small size fool you—there's a lot of power wrapped up in its small icon.

Note: And, if you have a large enough computer monitor, or are working with a dual monitor display, you can keep the program monitor in video mode and open the reference monitor panel to display the scopes full time in there.

What's the Reference Monitor?

It acts like a second program monitor

The reference monitor acts like a secondary program monitor. You can use it to compare different frames from the same sequence side by side, display scopes to color correct the image in the program monitor, or view the same frame using different viewing modes.

To open the reference monitor, select **Window > Reference Monitor.**

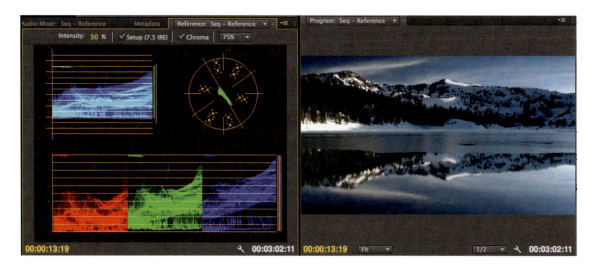

120

(Continued)

To gang (which means "connect") the reference monitor to the program monitor so that they both display the same frame in a clip or sequence, click the wrench icon in the reference monitor and select the top choice: **Gang to Program Monitor**.

If you don't gang the two monitors, you can easily display one image in the program monitor and a different image in the reference monitor.

Note: This is especially useful in a dual monitor setup so that you can always view the video scopes, by putting the reference monitor on the second computer display.

Full Screen Source or Program Monitors

Display your images full-screen with a click

Want to see either the source or program monitors full-screen?

The accent key (`) switches between the normal workspace and enlarging a single panel to fill the frame.

Control+`** enlarges the video in the source or program monitors so it fills the frame. (Type **Control+` to return to your normal workspace.)

Note: SD footage blown up to this size will look grainy and blurry. This technique is best used for HD video.

Fix It Quick

A fast keystroke to fix a file

Suddenly discover there's a problem in a file you need to fix?

No problem. Select the file in the Project panel and type **Command+E** (Mac OS) **Control+E** (Windows). The file instantly opens in the program that created it.

(Continued)

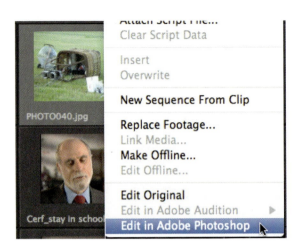

Except ... sometimes, an image file doesn't open in Photoshop, as you'd expect. That's because the file extension points to a different program.

To open an image file in Photoshop right-click the selected file in the Project panel and choose **Edit in Adobe Photoshop**. To fix problem audio in Audition, do the same thing, except select **Edit in Adobe Audition**.

As soon as you save the fixed file, Premiere updates itself with the latest version.

CHAPTER 6

Premiere Pro—Editing and Trimming

All the prep work is done, it's time to get down to the business of editing. The process is simple: decide what the next shot will be, select the part of the shot you want to use, and add the shot to the Timeline. Then, repeat. Over and over ... and over.

If projects only contained half-a-dozen clips, no one would worry about speed. However, most projects contain hundreds of clips—and speed is everything. Anytime you're not thinking creatively, you are wasting time. This chapter makes you faster so you can become more creative.

Name Your Sequence

Make your sequences easier to find

This is trick I first discovered when using Final Cut Pro, and it still works great in Premiere Pro.

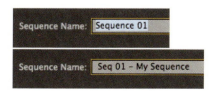

(Continued)

As you can see at the top of this screen shot, when you create a new sequence, Premiere cheerfully suggests naming your first sequence: "Sequence 01." This is, I'm sure, a very nice name. But not very useful.

Instead, as the bottom of the screen shot illustrates, I start all my sequence names with a space, followed by "Seq" then a number and a name. Because the Project panel always alphabetizes files, putting a space at the beginning of a sequence name bubbles all my sequences to the top so I don't have to hunt to find them.

The number allows me to control the display order of multiple sequences, as well as track which sequence version this is.

The dash appeals to the unfulfilled graphics designer within me.

And the sequence name is so I can remember what is in the sequence.

Note: When numbering sequences, I leave gaps between numbers—01, 05, 10, 15—this allows me to insert sequences without having to resort to "01aaaaaaa."

A Faster Way to Create a New Sequence

Drag and drop a clip to create and configure new sequence

It used to be that creating a new sequence was a multistep process. Now, you can create a new sequence and automatically configure it for your footage, all in one step.

Select a clip in the Project panel that is the video format you want to edit and drag it to the bottom of the Project panel and drop it on top of the **New Item** icon (second from right).

Almost instantly, this creates a new sequence and configures it to match the settings of the clip.

Another Way to Automatically Configure a Sequence

The first clip makes all the difference

When you edit a clip into an empty sequence using keyboard shortcuts or one of the edit buttons (Overwrite or Insert), the clip will automatically configure itself to match the sequence settings, even if the clip settings don't match the sequence settings.

However, when you *drag* a clip into an empty sequence, if the clip settings don't match the sequence settings, you'll see this dialog.

Change sequence settings. This changes the sequence to match the clip.

Keep existing settings. This alters the clip to match the sequence, which means the clip will need to render before final output. (This has no effect on the actual media file stored on your hard disk.)

If you don't know the video format you are editing, this is a simple way to make sure the sequence settings correctly match your clips.

What Is a Selected Track?

This term is used a lot; here's what it means

Throughout much of the rest of this book, the term "selected track," or "select a track," is used.

A selected track is one where the track header is a lighter gray. In this screen shot, video tracks 1 and 3 are selected, as is audio track 2.

You toggle whether a track is selected or not by clicking on the track header.

Note: You need to select tracks individually by clicking the headers. Shift-dragging, or other modifier keys to select multiple tracks won't work.

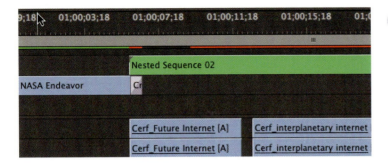

A Quick Way to Get Organized

Nesting allows you to treat a group of clips as a single clip

"Nesting" means to put one sequence into another sequence. This is a very useful technique to organize a Timeline, or gather a group of clips together as a single clip.

For instance, let's say I want to build a show master for final output. I've created each of the four acts in this thirty-minute program as a separate sequence in Premiere. Now, I want to combine each act into a single program, while also making sure that they appear in the right order.

Here's how.

Create a new sequence with the settings you want to use for output, then, open that sequence into the Timeline panel.

Drag each sequence from the Project panel into the Timeline in the order you want for playback. This is one way to nest sequences, and is very powerful for longer projects.

Note: A very useful technique is to gather a group of selected clips into a single collection called a "nest." In this case, select the clips you want to gather together and choose **Clip > Nest**.

The nice thing about nesting sequences is that you can treat them just like clips: they can be moved, trimmed, even have effects applied to the entire sequence.

To nest one sequence, say a show open, into another sequence, say the body of the show, simply select the sequence "Show Open" icon in the Project panel and drag it into the sequence containing the body of the show in the Timeline.

(Continued)

To edit or view the contents of a nest, double-click it in the Timeline. Any changes you make inside the nest are immediately reflected in the sequence that contains it.

A Hidden Way to Set the In and the Out

Save time, mark clips in the project panel

The only problem with using the Source monitor to set the In and the Out is that you first need to load the clip into the Source monitor. It would save a lot of time if we could mark the In and Out in the Project panel, without loading it anywhere.

In CS6 we can, and here's how:

1. Change the Project panel to Icon view, then select a clip in the Project panel.

2. Notice the gold bar at the bottom. That represents the mini-Timeline of the clip.

3. Click anywhere in the gold bar to move the mini-playhead and drag it where you want to set the In. The thumbnail will scroll to show you the frame you are selecting.

4. Type **I** to set the In.

5. Scroll the mini-playhead and type **O** to set the Out.

Note: If you need to change the size of your thumbnails, drag the thumbnail slider at the bottom of the Project panel. However, an even faster technique is to type **Shift+[** to make thumbnails smaller or **Shift+]** to make thumbnails bigger.

Sequence Your Clips

A fast way to add clips and transitions to a sequence

The Automate to Sequence button is a fast way to add a selected group of clips from the Project panel to the position of your playhead in the currently active Sequence.

Select your clips in the order in which you want them edited into the Timeline.

While you could drag them on top of the icon, it is faster just to click the icon to display the Automate to Sequence dialog.

Sequence Your Way to a Fast Montage

Use automate to sequence to create a montage, with transitions, in a hurry

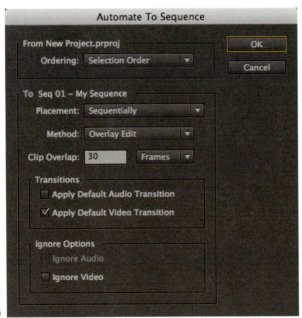

The pressure is on. You need to come up with an image montage like... now! And, it needs to include transitions!

Piece of cake.

Display your images as an image "storyboard" by clicking the Icon view icon in the lower left corner of the Project panel. Then, drag the clip thumbnails into the order you want—starting at the top left and going to the bottom right.

Select the clips you want to add to the Timeline and click the **Automate to Sequence** button.

In the dialog, you can determine the order the clips are edited into the sequence, where they are placed, whether this should be an overwrite or insert edit, and whether you want to add either audio or video transitions.

(Continued)

This is SO fast, you can create montages faster than real time.

Note: Remember, if you need to set Ins or Outs, you can do that directly in the thumbnail displayed in the Project panel, as mentioned earlier.

Figure Out Field Dominance

The world can't move to progressive video fast enough for me

When creating a new sequence, one of the most challenging areas is figuring out how to set field dominance. Field dominance is only used for interlaced video (including HD formats that end with the letter "i".)

When creating a new sequence, the Settings tab displays the Fields pop-up. Here are some quick rules:

- If you are using an existing preset, don't adjust this setting. Adjusting this setting is most relevant when creating a custom sequence.

- If you are shooting progressive video (HD formats that end with the letter "p") set this to **No Fields (Progressive Scan)**

- If you are shooting NTSC or PAL *DV* footage, set this to **Lower Field First**.

- If you are shooting NTSC or PAL *standard-definition* footage, set this to **Upper Field First**.

- If you are shooting HD footage, set this to **Upper Field First**.

If your images look blurry during movement, you've probably set this incorrectly. Create a new sequence and change the settings. Pick the one that looks the best during movement (images that don't move will always look good.)

Note: By the way, if you are trying to decide which video format to shoot—shoot progressive. It makes life much easier.

Configure Video Tracks

Save time—create new video tracks when you create your sequence

When creating a new sequence, save time by clicking the Tracks tab and specifying how many video tracks you need.

When you click **OK**, Premiere creates the sequence and the tracks you need all at once.

(I, uh, may have gotten a bit carried away in this screen shot by creating thirty tracks. However, because Premiere allows us to create up to ninety-nine tracks, feel free to use as many as you need.)

Configure Audio Tracks

CS6 Makes audio configuration a lot easier

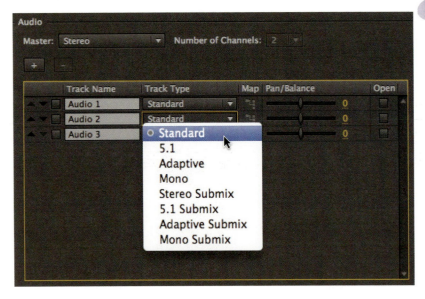

In the past, Premiere Pro required that all audio configurations be specified before editing audio into them. For editors new to Premiere, this caused a fair amount of confusion.

Now, applying the Standard setting to an audio track means that the track will automatically adjust to whatever audio elements are dropped into it.

However, if you need specific settings, say for surround sound or submixes, you can explicitly set them here.

Change Sequence Settings

Not all settings can be changed, unless ...

If, in the middle of an edit, you realize that you need to change your sequence settings, select the Timeline panel, then go to **Sequence > Sequence Settings**.

Some settings, like timecode and audio display, are easily changed. However, many of the settings are not changeable because clips are edited into the sequence. So, to change these sequence settings, create a new sequence and make whatever settings changes are necessary. Then, open it in the Timeline.

Finally, copy and paste clips from the old sequence into the new sequence.

Note: Changing settings like timebase, frame size, or pixel aspect ratio will significantly alter how your clips look. So, if you change these settings, expect to make adjustments to your edit.

Audio Track Editing

In Premiere Pro CS5.5, before we could add audio to a track, we needed to configure the track as either mono or stereo.

No more!

The default track setting, Standard, means that when you edit or drag audio into a track, it will automatically accept either mono or stereo clips. Even better, we can now add *both* mono and stereo clips to the *same* track!

(Continued)

Note: For other audio track types, such as 5.1 surround or adaptive, the track needs to be preset for that format before editing audio into the track.

Importing DSLR Video Sources

Most DSLR cameras create quicktime movies by default

DSLR cameras generally create QuickTime movies that can be easily imported directly into Premiere for editing. Here's the process:

1 Copy the entire contents of your camera's memory card to a hard drive. You should back up at least one more copy to another drive before you erase the memory card. Make sure at least one of the hard drives you copy the card's media to is fast enough for video editing.

2 In Adobe Premiere Pro, select the Media Browser panel. If it's not visible, choose **Window > Media Browser**. If necessary, drag the edge of the panel to make the Media Browser larger so that you can see thumbnails. (Or, press the **Accent** (`` ` ``) key to zoom the selected panel full-screen.)

3 Browse to the folder containing the media files. You only need to select the folder, not the contents inside it. The Media Browser will show a thumbnail of the footage, if the format supports it, and the name of each shot. Use Hover scrub to review the action in a clip.

4 Select the clips you want to import in the Media Browser.

5 Choose **File > Import > From Media Browser (Option+Command+I— or—Alt+Control+I)**. Adobe Premiere Pro imports the selected footage as individual clips into the Project panel.

Make Your Mark

Save time—set ins and outs faster

Editing is a repetitive series of tasks. Determine your next clip. Set the In. Set the Out. Edit to the Timeline. Repeat. Repeat again. And again. The hard part in this process is the creative challenge of figuring out the next shot. Editing clips to the Timeline needs to be fast and simple. That's where these shortcuts can help.

Every second you save in marking (setting the In and Out) and editing a clip adds up into hours saved over the course of a project. So practice using these keyboard shortcuts and get some of your life back.

These keyboard shortcuts work in either the Source, Program, or Timeline panels.

Shortcut	Shortcut	What it does
CS5.5	CS6	
I	I	Sets the In
G	Shift+I	Jumps the playhead to the In
D	Option(Alt)+I	Deletes the In
O	O	Sets the Out
W	Shift+O	Jumps the playhead to the Out
F	Option(Alt)+O	Deletes the Out
G	Option(Alt)+X	Deletes both the In and the Out

Note: The CS5.5 keyboard shortcuts were designed to lie under the fingers of the left hand, which allows you to keep your right hand on the mouse, while the left hand works the keyboard. The CS6 shortcuts emulate many of the shortcuts used by Final Cut Pro 7.

Flashes of Black Will Get You Fired

Find and remove small timeline gaps, which cause black flashes

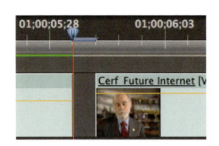

Nothing says "Bad Editing Done Here" than short flashes of black where edit points are supposed to be. But, sometimes those suckers are only one frame long and impossible to see when you are zoomed back on the Timeline.

Gaps between B-roll clips are expected. But not, generally, in V1—the main Timeline track. Premiere makes it easy to find those microscopic gaps:

● Select **Sequence > Go to Gap > Next in track**. You also have the option to find the next gap in the sequence, but far too often that jumps to a gap between B-roll clips, which is quite normal. I prefer to look for gaps in the main V1 track.

● To remove a gap, click the gap to select it, and press the big Delete key. Poof! Gone.

While the default keyboard shortcuts for Premiere don't have a keyboard shortcut to find the next gap, you can easily create one. In fact, using a custom shortcut will *really* speed finding these pesky critters.

Note: Why emphasize the "big Delete key" (the key two keys above the Return key)? Because the **Delete** and **DEL** keys are programmed differently. And, besides, the DEL key doesn't exist on many laptops.

Why Create Subclips?

Subclips make a portion of a clip act like a complete clip

Subclips allow you to break a long clip into shorter clips, which, essentially, creates new stand-alone clips in the Project panel, without duplicating any media. The difference between a subclip and a clip with an In and Out is that the subclip acts as an independent clip.

136

(Continued)

Creating subclips is a useful technique if you are capturing long sections from tape and want to break that single capture into more manageable chunks. Subclipping allows you to subdivide a clip, without using any more media space.

Subclipping is also useful for some effects that use a clip as an input source–stereoscopic 3D video is a current example. These effects base their timing on the start of the clip, not the position of the In or the Out.

To create a subclip:

● Load a clip into the Source window

● Mark the In and Out points

● Choose **Clip > Make Subclip**

● Give the subclip a name and click **OK**.

● The clip is automatically added to the same bin as the source clip.

There is no limit to the number of subclips you can make from a single master clip and more than one subclip can reference the same media.

L-Cuts and J-Cuts

Split edits are a good way to hide an edit

Sometimes, the best way to hide an edit is to have the audio and video edit points occur at different times in the Timeline. This allows the viewer to see one thing, while hearing another; dramatic editing uses this type of cut frequently.

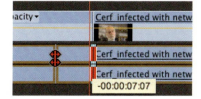

(Continued)

There are two types of split edits: an L-cut and a J-cut. (These are named for the shape the edits form in the Timeline.) In an L-cut, the video edit point precedes the audio edit. In a J-cut, the audio edit precedes the video.

These split-edits are especially helpful when editing dialogue because they give the editor better control over pacing and reaction shots, or to hide a continuity error.

Here's how to create a split edit:

- Select the Rolling Edit tool (**N**) and move it to an edit point.

- **Option-click** (Mac OS) or **Alt-click** (Windows) on the edit point you want to adjust - video or audio. (Most often, I use this technique to adjust the video edit.)

- For example, drag the video edit point left in the timeline to create an L-cut or right to create a J-cut. You can preview the outgoing and incoming frames in the Program monitor while dragging.

Note: To select both audio tracks, **Option (Alt)** click to select the first audio edit point, then hold down the **Shift** key and click to select the second audio edit point.

Clean Up Your Timeline

Stay organized and efficient

A clean timeline speeds editing. Here are a few quick tips to keep your sequences neat and tidy.

- **Use workspaces**. Adobe has created useful workspaces for Audio, Color Correction, Editing, Effects, and Metalogging. Choose **Window > Workspace** and then select the desired task. You can also create new workspaces or reset an existing workspace to its default view.

138

(Continued)

- **Delete unused tracks**. Right-click a track header in the Timeline and choose **Delete Tracks**. In the pop-up window, you can choose to remove a specific track, or all empty audio and video tracks. (Or, choose **Sequence > Delete Tracks** to get to the same dialog.)

- **Rename tracks**. You can right-click an audio or video track header to rename it. This can make organization easier (especially for complex audio mixes).

- **Condense clips using nests**. If your sequence contains multiple layers of clips, condense them into a single, yet still editable, Timeline clip using a nest. A nest is a collection of clips grouped into a sequence that is contained in another sequence. Select the clips you want to group and choose **Clip > Nest** (or right-click the selected clips and select **Nest**).

Edit Clips in Timecode Order

(Or any other order, for that matter)

[This tip was taken from a tip at **DVinfo.net**.]

Here's a fast way to edit clips into the timeline in the order of their timecode. This is useful when you want to build a selects reel in the order the clips were shot:

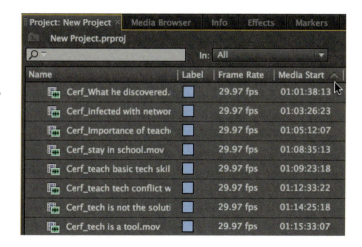

- In the Project panel, click the **Media Start** column header, the **Video In** header, or any other column header in the panel.

- This sorts all Project panel entries in either ascending or descending order for that column. (To reverse the sort order, click the column header again.)

- Then select the clips you want to edit as a group and drag them to the Timeline, or the Automate to Sequence icon.

(Continued)

139

The clips edit to the Timeline in the order they were selected. You can also use this method to organize clips by duration, file name, or any other Project panel column.

Slicing Your Clips

A fast way to slice and dice your clips

Trimming, along with shot selection, is at the heart of editing. Anything that speeds up trimming is a good thing. So here are some quick keyboard shortcuts for slicing and dicing your clips.

Command (Control)+K: Split all clips with a selected track header, at the position of the playhead.

Shift+Command(Control)+K: Split all tracks at the position of the playhead, whether the track header is selected or not.

You can also use these keyboard shortcuts to slice clips in real time during playback.

Note: On some Windows systems, **Control+K** cuts all clips on all tracks.

Perform an Extend Edit in Real Time

We could do this in CS5.5, but it's much easier in CS6

An extend edit is one in which the edit point moves to the location of the playhead with a keyboard shortcut, essentially this is a high-speed roll trim.

In Premiere CS 5.5, we could not directly select an edit point in the Timeline, so we used two commands to perform an extend edit: one to move the edit point forward to the playhead and another to move the edit point backward to the

(Continued)

playhead. These are called **Extend Previous Edit to Playhead** (**E**) and **Extend Next Edit to Playhead** (**Shift+E**).

To perform an extend edit in CS5.5, do the following:

1 Target the tracks you wish to effect in the extend edit.

2 Park the playhead where you want to extend (roll) the edit point to.

3 Press **E** to extend the previous edit to the playhead.

4 Press **Shift+E** to extend the next edit to the playhead.

5 The edit point instantly snaps to the playhead.

In Premiere CS6, this is *much* easier. We can use either the Ripple Edit tool (**B**) or the Rolling Edit tool (**N**) to select an edit point, then press **E** to jump the selected edit point to the position of the playhead.

What's even nicer is that we can now do this in real time! Play the playhead and type **E** where you want the edit point to jump.

Poof! Rippling and rolling in real time.

Get Rid of the Garbage

Ripple trim to the position of the playhead

If you find yourself constantly trimming tops and tails, there are four hidden shortcuts in CS6 that provide a fast way to select or trim the heads and tails of a clip. Except, these are hidden in the Keyboard Shortcuts menu; they aren't actually connected to anything. You need to assign keyboard shortcuts to get these to work.

(Continued)

Choose **Premiere Pro > Keyboard Shortcuts** and search for "Ripple."

***Ripple Trim Next Edit to Playhead**. This trims the tail of a clip to the playhead position.

***Ripple Trim Previous Edit to Playhead**. This trims the head of a clip to the playhead position.

Or, if you are more the meditative type who needs to reflect on your edits, try:

- Select Nearest Edit Point as Ripple In.
- Select Nearest Edit Point as Ripple Out.

Now that you have it selected, you can use the keyboard to quickly relocate the edit.

Note: A ripple trim adjusts either the In or the Out of a clip, a Roll trim adjusts both.

The Trim Monitor in CS5.5

This allows fast and precise trimming of clips

Here's how to work with the Trim Monitor in Premiere CS5.5:

1. Park the playhead on or near any edit point.

2. Press the **T** key, the Trim Monitor Launches.

3. Press the Spacebar to begin looping playback. Audio and video will playback repeatedly. This allows you to figure out what you want to do.

4. To ripple trim the edit point, first select the correct side of the edit point you wish to trim. For a roll trim, select both sides of the edit point.

   - To set up a roll trim: press **Option+1** (**Alt+1** for Windows).

142

(Continued)

- To set up a ripple trim for the outgoing shot: press **Option+2** (**Alt+2** for Windows).

- To set up a ripple trim for the incoming shot: press **Option+3** (**Alt+3** for Windows).

- Once you have set up the trim mode, you should see blue bars above and below the clip(s) you wish to trim.

5 After the mode is set, choose the amount of frames you wish to trim.

- To trim backward by one frame, press **Option+Left Arrow** (**Alt+Left Arrow**).

- To trim backward by multiple frames, press **Option+Shift+Left Arrow** (**Alt+Shift+Left Arrow**).

- To trim forward by one frame, press **Option+Right Arrow** (**Alt+Right Arrow**).

- To trim forward by multiple frames, press **Option+Shift+Right Arrow** (**Alt+Shift+Right Arrow**).

6 Press the Spacebar once more to begin looping playback. Evaluate the cut and repeat steps 4 and 5, if necessary.

7 If you are satisfied with the cut, move to the next cut by pressing the **Page Down** key. Press the **Page Up** key to move to the previous cut.

8 When done, close the Trim Monitor by pressing **Command+W** (**Control+W**).

Note: The Trim Monitor was replaced with all new trimming tools in Premiere CS6, which I cover next.

Turning on Trim Mode in CS6

The new trim mode allows much more flexibility in trimming edit points

The Trim mode is new with Premiere Pro CS6. It allows a more visual way to trim, along with the ability to trim clips in real-time.

There are three ways to turn on Trim mode (and simply selecting an edit point isn't one of them). Do one of the following:

- Double-click any edit point with any trimming tool, which automatically moves the playhead to that edit point.

- Use **Sequence > Edit Trim** to switch the Program Monitor into Trim mode. If you don't have an edit point selected, the playhead moves to the nearest edit point on a selected track and selects the edit point.

- Use the Ripple or Roll tool to marquee select one or more edit points, which automatically moves the playhead to the nearest selected edit point and opens the Trim mode window.

To exit Trim mode, do one of the following:

- Move the playhead so it is no longer on the selected edit point.

- Select or move anything that isn't an edit point.

- Select another sequence.

Do Your Trimming in Real Time

Create ripple or roll trims in real time using the keyboard

144

You can trim your edits in real time using this very cool technique.

(Continued)

- Enter Trim mode, say by double-clicking an edit point. This also jumps the playhead to the selected edit point.

- Press the **J** key to play backward or **L** to play forward.

- When you press the **K** key, the selected edit point will immediately jump to the position of the playhead.

Trim Multiple Edit Points At Once

This is SO cool—trim multiple edit points at the same time

With the CS6 release, you can now select multiple edit points in the same Timeline and trim them.

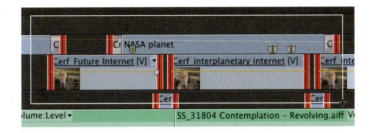

Think of creating a montage of video images that edits with the beat of the music. Except, after editing the entire sequence, the client decides to replace the music with something a bit faster. You've got all the shots in the right order, but the edits are no longer in the right place.

This is now an easy problem to solve. This technique allows you to trim all selected edit point by the same amount, using the same trimming tool.

- Select the trimming tool you want to use—Ripple or Rolling Edit.

- Drag a marquee around all the edit points you want to trim. If you need to add more, **Shift-click** to select them.

- Drag the trim tool to adjust the first edit. All selected edit points will be adjusted by the same amount in the same direction.

Pretty amazing!

Trimming Keyboard Shortcuts

Trim faster by using keyboard shortcuts

Premiere's trimming functions were totally rewritten for the CS6 release. There are now three types of trims:

- **Trim**, which moves either the In or Out of a clip and leaves a gap between two clips. No clip shifting occurs.

- **Ripple** trim, which moves either the In or Out, and shifts all downstream clips so there is no gap

- **Roll** trim, which moves both the In and the Out such that the clips stay in sync and there's no gap. No clip shifting occurs.

Trims and Ripple trims are generally done to get two clips in sync. A Roll trim is used to change the timing of the edit, without damaging the sync.

Use the Selection tool (**V**) to Trim In or Trim Out. When hovering over an unselected edit point, press **Command** (**Control**) to change to the Ripple In, Ripple Out, or Roll tool, depending upon which side of the edit the cursor is located.

Note: While pressing the Command key, you can also activate the Roll tool by clicking directly on the edit point. Click on either side of an unselected edit point to activate the Ripple tool for that side.

Use the Ripple tool (**B**) to Ripple In or Ripple Out. Press **Command** (**Control**) to change to the Roll or Trim In / Trim Out tool, depending upon which side of the edit point the cursor is located.

Trimming One Side of a Linked Clip

Trim just the audio or video of a linked clip using this technique

If you want to select just one side of a linked clip, such as just the video or just the audio, a modifier key will do the trick. Select the trimming tool you want to use:

- **Selection** to simply move the end of a clip.

- **Ripple** to move the end of a clip and shift all downstream slips horizontally so there is no gap.

- **Rolling** to move the edit point without moving any clips.

Use **Option** (**Alt**) to select just the video or just the audio of a linked clip.

Use **Shift** to add or remove other edit points so you can trim all selected edit points at the same time.

For example, combine **Option** (**Alt**) with **Shift** to select multiple video-only edit points.

Note: You can also select the beginning or end of a gap in the Timeline using this same technique.

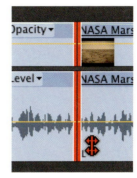 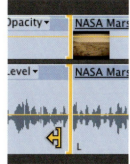

Red and Yellow Are Not the Same Thing

The color of an edit point indicates the trim mode

Once an edit point is selected, Premiere Pro indicates what you are about to do by the color and shape of the selected edit point.

- Red brackets indicate a trim.

- Yellow brackets indicate a ripple trim.

- Red bar indicated a roll trim.

(Continued)

147

You can toggle between the Ripple and Rolling Edit trim tools by pressing **Command** (**Control**).

Trimming Keyboard Shortcuts

Menu shortcuts help select the right edit point

There are new trimming choices that can help select the edit point you want to trim. However, these are not available in a menu or an existing keyboard shortcut—to activate them, go to **Premiere Pro > Keyboard Shortcuts** and search for "Select," then, create your own keyboard shortcuts.

Shortcut	What It Does
Go To Next Selected Edit Point	Jumps playhead to next selected edit point to the right.
Go to Previous Selected Edit Point	Jumps playhead to next selected edit point to the left.
Select Nearest Edit Point as Ripple In	Deselects any selected edit point, jumps the playhead to the nearest edit point, and selects it as a Ripple In.
Select Nearest Edit Point as Ripple Out	Deselects any selected edit point, jumps the playhead to the nearest edit point, and selects it as a Ripple Out.
Select Nearest Edit Point as Roll	Deselects any selected edit point, jumps the playhead to the nearest edit point, and selects it as a Roll.
Select Nearest Edit Point as Trim In	Deselects any selected edit point, jumps the playhead to the nearest edit point, and selects it as a Trim In.
Select Nearest Edit Point as Trim Out	Deselects any selected edit point, jumps the playhead to the nearest edit point, and selects it as a Trim Out.

Theoretically**, Control+T** should toggle between selecting the Ripple Out, Ripple In, Trim Out, Trim In, and Roll trimming tools, in that order. However, although it is listed as a Keyboard shortcut, it is not working in the current version. I expect Adobe to fix this shortly.

Trim Using Numeric Offsets

This is the fastest way to move a precise amount

The nice thing about dragging an edit point is that is it fast. The problem is that it isn't accurate. If you want speed with accuracy, using numeric offsets is the way to go. (Personally, this is one of my favorite ways to trim.)

- Select an edit point (In, Out, or both.)

- On the keypad, all the way to the right of your keyboard, type **+** followed by the number of frames you want to trim, followed by **ENTER**. (For example, **+15 [ENTER]** moves the selected edit point fifteen frames to right.)

- To move the edit point to the right, type **+** followed by a number. To move to the left, type **-**.

- Enter any number from one to ninety-nine, and Premiere will treat all the numbers as frames. To enter timecode for larger values, type numbers for hours.minutes.seconds.frames, where each pair of numbers is separated by a period.

Multicam Keyboard Shortcuts

New keyboard shortcuts for multicam editing

The new multicam editing feature in Premiere Pro allows you to edit many more cameras than ever before. And, using the default keyboard shortcuts, you can easily edit between nine different angles. (You can also create your own keyboard shortcuts for another seven angles for a total of sixteen!)

(Continued)

There are two options: to select an angle, which replaces the angle under the playhead with the new angle, or to cut to an angle, which forces an edit point at the position of the playhead and changes the angle of the downstream (to the right) clip.

Task	Mac	Windows
Select a camera angle	1—9	1—9
Cut to a different angle	Command+1 - 9	Control+1 - 9

In this example, to select camera angle 2, press **2**. To cut to camera angle 2, type **Command+2 (Control+2)**

CHAPTER 7

Premiere Pro—Audio

The best way to improve the quality of your picture is to improve the quality of your sound. Premiere Pro CS6 contains some strong audio tools. However, for industry-leading audio repair and mixing, Premiere makes it easy to send projects to Adobe Audition, which we cover in the next chapter.

This chapter helps you make the most of the audio tools in Premiere itself.

The Number #1 Audio Rule

Audio levels must never exceed 0 dB

This rule isn't really a Power Tip—but it is so important that it bears restating.

Audio levels must *never* exceed 0 dB. Not once, not for a little bit, not even though you think they should. Never. What makes this challenging is that audio gain is additive, the more clips you have playing at the same time, the louder your master audio levels will be.

Audio peaks that exceed 0 dB are indicated by red bars at the top of the vertical Audio Meters, or the right side when meters are horizontal.

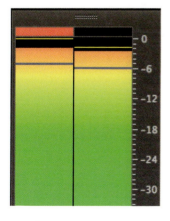

(Continued)

The reason for this rule is that audio levels greater than zero—indicated by a red bar at the top of the audio meters—will distort when exported from Premiere Pro. And distorted audio sounds awful, cannot be fixed, and makes children run screaming from the room.

Pay attention to your audio and keep your levels under control.

Hey, Premiere Pro Lets Me Set Audio Levels Over 0 dB!

Well, the difference is relative

There are two kinds of audio levels: absolute and relative.

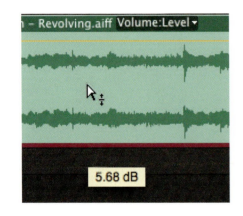

Audio meters display absolute levels. This is a display of the precise audio level that your clip or sequence is currently playing. These are the levels that must not exceed 0 dB.

Clips, tracks, and the audio mixer display relative levels. With relative levels, 0 dB refers to the level of the audio *at which it was recorded.* (Folks that have been mixing audio for a long time call this point "Unity.") So, as you raise the level of a clip, you are increasing the level of the clip, compared to the level at which it was recorded. The total level—the absolute level—is displayed in the audio meters.

Most dialog is recorded softer than you want for the final mix. (Recording a bit low avoids distortion in case an actor suddenly starts shouting.) So we generally increase the level of dialog, compared to the level at which it was recorded.

Most music is recorded very loud, so, again generally, we decrease the level of music as compared to the level at which it was recorded.

All these relative changes are reflected in the master audio levels for the entire edited project and displayed in the Audio Meters.

The Concept of Checkerboarding

Checkerboarding is the process of grouping similar audio on the same track

When I first started using the computer to edit, I considered audio to be a jigsaw puzzle. I tried to cram as many clips onto as few tracks as possible. This worked, but when I went back to a project later, I had no clue where I managed to put stuff.

Premiere doesn't really care where you put audio clips anymore. So, the goal is to put them in such a location that simplifies finding, editing, and mixing clips.

For me, I follow the following track layout table when I'm editing. I've been using this approach for the last ten years. The benefit is that anytime I open an older project, I know exactly where my audio is, without having to waste any time.

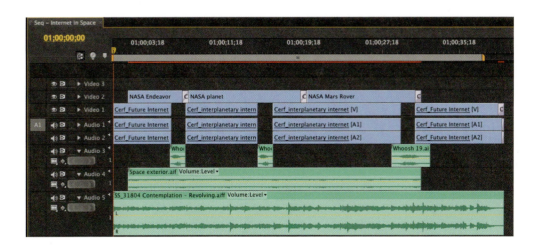

Track	What Goes On It
A1	Sync dialog or interviews from women (mono)
A2	Sync dialog or interviews from men (mono)
A3/A4	Natural sound from B-roll clips (stereo)
A5	Narration (mono)
A6—8	Sound effects—both mono and stereo
A9	Music clip 1 (stereo)
A10	Music clip 2 (stereo)

As a note, I make a point to record all dialog, interview audio, and narration as either mono, or dual channel mono, audio. This provides much more flexibility in mixing than a stereo clip.

If I need more than three sound effects tracks, I add them after the narration and before the music clips in the Timeline.

Also, to give me the ability to slowly fade out one music clip, while quickly fading in a second music clip, I put my music on alternating tracks.

By using checkerboarding, whether I mix my audio in Premiere Pro—which I rarely do—or Audition—which I almost always do—my audio is ready to mix without me having to do any additional audio setup.

Note: To save space, if I don't have any narration or sound effects clips, for example, I don't leave a blank track, I just pull up all lower tracks.

A Follow-On Note to Checkerboarding

Here's why checkerboarding helps

Putting similar audio on the same track enables the use of common track effects to manage one type of audio. Otherwise, you end up applying duplicate filters/effects to each clip separately which is very wasteful of CPU processing.

(Continued)

156

I use track effects for multiple source interviews—for example, I'll create separate EQ/compression settings for each individual location/voice and apply it to a track. Say, one track for men's voices and a second track for women. It then becomes easy to position the appropriate audio on the appropriately prepped track.

It's a Small Thing But ...

How do you display audio waveforms?

You can stop laughing. When I first started using Premiere, I couldn't figure out how to display the audio waveforms.

Click the small, white, right-pointing triangle to expand the track and display audio waveforms.

To make the entire track larger, drag the black horizontal line that separates track headers up or down. Larger tracks allow you to be more precise in setting levels or pan.

To adjust audio levels, drag the yellow line in the middle of the audio clip up or down.

Note: For more precision in setting levels or pan use the adjustments in the Effects Controls panel.

Displaying Waveforms in the Source Monitor

By default, premiere pro displays video, not audio

By default, Premiere displays video in the Source monitor. Most of the time, this is great. However, for those situations where you would rather see the audio, right-click the image in the Source monitor and select **Display Mode > Audio Waveform**.

(Continued)

157

To reset the Source monitor back to video, select **Display Mode > Composite Video**.

There's no default keyboard shortcut for this, but you can create one. To find the menu choice in Keyboard Shortcuts, search for "waveform."

Setting the Right Levels for Your Mix

The term "best levels" causes bar fights

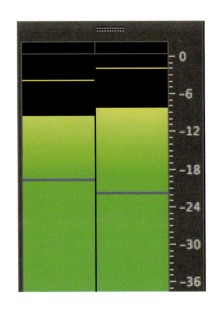

Audio levels are additive. That means that the more clips you have playing at the same time, the louder your whole mix gets. (Audio old-timers called this "summing" the tracks.) Keeping in mind that your total levels can't exceed 0 dB, where do you set levels?

This is an easy question to ask, but difficult to answer; because different regions of the world measure audio levels differently and different distribution formats require different levels.

Premiere Pro measures audio peaks using a scale called dBFS (decibels Full Scale). However, many broadcasters are more concerned with average audio levels (also called RMS) than peak levels. Also, new standards in the European Union requires measuring audio levels in LUFS, which are also a form of average audio levels.

While both peaks and averages are measured in dB, they yield different numbers, which causes no end of confusion.

If you are mixing for the web, I recommend that peaks for your total mix bounce around −3 dB.

If you are mixing for delivery to other formats, I strongly recommend you ask the people who are receiving your files where they want the audio levels set.

158

(Continued)

Note: However, this is not always good advice. A friend was mixing a project for a large national cable company, which shall remain nameless. He was provided a twelve-page written description containing video specification requirements, but not a word on audio. He called their tech center to ask for specifics and, when finally transferred to the "engineer in charge," was told: "just set your audio levels as you usually do."

Second Note: There's a special measurement in Audition called "Amplitude Statistics." I talk about it in the next chapter. This feature, alone, makes learning Audition worth the effort.

Customize Your Audio Meters

Make your audio meters more accurate and more flexible

When setting audio levels, always trust your meters and not your ears. The CS6 release of Premiere Pro redesigned the Audio Meters to be scalable, more accurate, and react similarly to the audio meters in Audition. (Audition, by the way, is a stalwart in radio broadcasting.)

Meters can now display horizontally or vertically, scale as necessary, and meter both the Source and Program monitor content.

To change the size of the meters, drag the black dividing line along the edge of the meters.

Right-click inside the meters to:

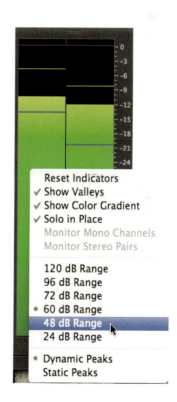

- Reset the red clip indicators
- **Show Valleys**. This highlights (ah, "lowlights?") the softest part of the audio for the last few seconds
- **Show Color Gradient**. This changes the color display of the audio levels as they get closer to 0 dB from green to yellow to red.

(Continued)

- Change range options to select the decibel range appropriate to your project

- **Display Dynamic Peaks**. This highlights the loudest portion of your audio and continuously resets the peak after three seconds.

- **Static Peaks**. This highlights the loudest portion of your audio and holds that display until reset or you restart playback. This is the best way to measure the absolute loudest peak during playback.

Creating Audio Clip Keyframes

Keyframes allow us to vary audio levels during playback

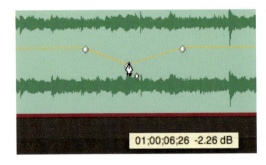

01;00;06;26 -2.26 dB

To change the audio level for an entire clip, drag the horizontal yellow line in the middle of the clip up or down.

However, sometimes you need to make one portion of a clip louder or softer without adjusting the entire clip. This is easy to do using keyframes.

A keyframe is a "point of change during playback." And, we always work with keyframes in pairs; there's a starting position and an ending position. A single keyframe, by itself, does nothing. Keyframes are the prime mover for animating both visual effects and audio levels.

To set keyframes, select the Pen tool **(P)** and click the yellow line where you want to start adjusting the volume. Next, click the yellow link to add a second keyframe where you want the adjustment to end.

Drag a keyframe up or down to adjust the gain setting for that keyframe. Drag it from side-to-side to adjust its position. (Once you start dragging in one direction—say, vertically—Premiere prevents you from moving in a different direction—say, horizontally.)

(Continued)

In the screen shot above, I'm using three keyframes to lower the volume from keyframe 1 to 2, then raise it back to its normal level from keyframe 2 to 3. While I'm using three keyframes, when setting or adjusting keyframes is always easiest to think of them in pairs—a starting and ending position.

Use Beziér Curves to Remove Sharp Corners

All audio keyframes can be smoothed using curves

Sometimes, you don't want abrupt changes in your audio. Adding a curve is easy, and, even better, you have control over the shape of these curves.

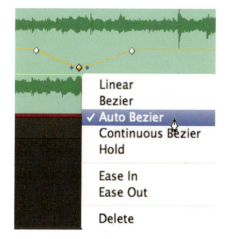

Right-click any keyframe and select the curve shape you want. My suggestion, if you are new to audio, is to select **Auto Beziér**. This provides a smooth curve which you can shape further, if you wish.

To return a curved keyframe to a corner, select **Linear**.

To delete a keyframe, select **Delete**.

To adjust the shape of a curve, drag one of the small handles on either side of the keyframe. However, for most audio, the default shape will be fine. Making these curve adjustments is more the province of visual effects than audio.

Note: Clicking a keyframe while holding the **Command** (**Control**) key will also cycle though these shape options, and it only requires one click to select **Auto-Beziér**, which eliminates a menu.

Rescuing an Out-of-Sync Clip

Finding and fixing out-of-sync clips is easy … just take control

If the audio and video of a linked clip gets out of sync, red numbers appear at the left edge of the affected clips indicating the time shift.

That indicates that for some reason, such as an incredible harmonic disconvergence or wild quirk of fate, your audio and video, which are supposed to be in sync, have gone astray.

Premiere uses timecode to keep audio and video clips in sync. And, most of the time, it does a great job. However, sometimes, the audio and video of a linked clip get out of sync. The most common causes of this condition are trimming a synced clip where one of the tracks is locked, or moving the audio without also moving the video.

When this dire event happens, red numbers at the left end of both clips indicate that clips are out of sync. To fix this problem, right-click directly on the red numbers in the clip. I generally recommend resetting the audio clip, but using either the audio or video will work.

- **Move Into Sync**, *moves* the clip you click instantly back into sync with its other half.

- **Slip into Sync**, *slips* the contents of the clip you click until the contents of both the audio and video are in sync.

In most situations, Move Into Sync is the best choice.

Note: In order for this technique to work, there needs to be some overlap between the two out-of-sync clips. If there isn't any overlap, well, um, good luck, because the red numbers won't appear.

Premiere Can Edit Compressed Audio Files

WAV or AIF is higher quality, but compressed files are welcome

There's a reason uncompressed audio was invented: it is faster, easier, and more accurate to edit. Both AIF and WAV files contain uncompressed audio.

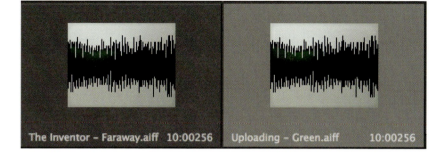

However, you don't need to convert compressed audio files. Just like Audition, Premiere will uncompress these files and store them in a temp file, so that during playback, Premiere is reading uncompressed audio data for maximum efficiency. There's only a processing hit when you first open the file, but that's done in the background so you can keep working.

As a general rule, converting audio files can never restore the material that was discarded during the original compression stage. What you are doing, instead, is converting the audio into a format that is easier to edit.

Compressed audio is ideal for posting to the web; however, they will be converted when you use them for editing.

What's a PEK File?

Is it the same as a PKF?

Premiere analyzes audio data, such as peaks and frequency, and stores it in a PEK file. PEK files are stored in a central location on your computer. These files are created automatically by Premiere when you first import a media file containing audio. There is one PEK file for each audio file.

(Continued)

PKF files are created automatically by Audition to track similar data about audio. However, PKF files are stored with the source clip. There is one PKF file for every audio file. Unfortunately, Audition can't read PEK files and Premiere can't read PKF files.

By contrast, you don't really need to worry about these. While both Audition and Premiere use these to display audio files quickly, if, for some reason, they accidentally get erased, Premiere will automatically rebuild them when needed.

Standard is the New Standard

The default timeline audio track type has changed

In Premiere CS5.5, stereo was the default audio track format. This caused all kinds of hassle when we needed to work with both mono *and* stereo files.

With CS6, Adobe changed the default setting to Standard.

What this means is that now you can use either mono or stereo audio in a track, without having to specify the audio format of the track first. Also, when you add new tracks to your Timeline, the new tracks will use Standard settings as well.

A couple of notes:

● Mono tracks are still available, but no longer default to multi-channel mono sequences.

● A Standard audio track will not accept 5.1 surround or adaptive audio clips. These require customizing your audio track settings.

Separate a Stereo Audio Track Into Two Mono Clips

Here's an easy way to separate a stereo pair into two mono clips

You were just handed an interview where the interviewer is on one channel and the guest is on the second channel. However, the clip was recorded and ingested as a stereo clip. How do you separate a stereo clip into two discrete mono clips?

In Premiere Pro CS5.5 and CS6, it is easier to separate the audio into two discreet clips (called "dual-channel mono"), rather than a stereo pair, *before* editing them to the Timeline. Separating interview tracks this way is almost always a good idea because it is easier to control a mono clip for pan and volume than a stereo clip.

Note: You can create this separation as a default in **Preferences > Audio** by changing the settings for **Default Audio Tracks**.

To create a dual-channel mono clip from a stereo clip:

- In the Project panel, select the clips you want to separate into individual audio channels.

- Right-click and select **Modify > Audio Channels**.

- In the dialog that appears, set the Preset from **Stereo** to **Mono** and Premiere will automatically display two mono tracks in the Project panel instead of one stereo track.

- Edit the track you want into the Timeline as normal.

(Continued)

Note: I strongly recommend recording interviews as a mono clips, or, if you have an interviewer and a guest, as two-channel mono where each speaker is on their own track. The ability to control each track separately makes mono audio far more preferable for editing and mixing than trying to edit a stereo pair.

What To Do With A Stereo Clip That Has Audio in Only One Track

Here are two options for handling stereo clips with only one audio track

In the last example, we had two speakers on two different channels of a stereo clip. In this example, the interviewer used only one mic and both she and the guest are on the same channel.

How do you remove the audio channel that you don't need from a stereo recording?

In Premiere Pro CS5.5 there's a way to combine both channels:

- Select the clip in the Project panel.

- Right-click and select **Audio > Fill Left** or **Audio > Fill Right**. This copies the contents of one audio channel into the other. Fill Left means taking the left channel and copying it to the right channel, which might seem backward to its description. Fill Right does the opposite.

- If you originally recorded only one channel, fill duplicates the channel you're copying. Although it doesn't create a stereo separation out of the one channel, it will give you sound from both channels instead of just one. This avoids having to convert the stereo clip to a mono clip.

(Continued)

In Premiere Pro CS6, you have more options:

- Select the clip in the Project panel.

- Right-click and select **Modify > Audio Channels**.

- At the top, set the Preset to **Mono**.

- Enter the number of audio tracks you want to create. I strongly prefer keeping a mono clip as a single audio track, rather than convert to stereo.

- In the pop-up at the bottom, select whether you want to hear the left or right channel. For dual-channel audio, Channel 1 is equivalent to left and Channel 2 is equivalent to right.

Note: This won't affect any clips already edited into the Timeline.

Surround is a Special Case

Surround audio needs its own track

If you are importing a surround 5.1 mix, and you want to retain the surround mix in the clip, you need to create a new 5.1 track.

If, on the other hand, you don't need the surround mix, you can either import it as a mono clip, or remap it into six mono channels, which is called a multi-channel mono track mix.

Note: Surround audio in Premiere is displayed differently than you might expect. For some inscrutable reason, Premiere uses a 5.1 channel order of "L R Ls Rs C LFE" and not the standard ITU layout, which is "L R C LFE Ls Rs." You may notice the channel layout is displayed incorrectly in clips and in the meters, but is displayed correctly in Audition. Premiere CS6 doesn't modify the file, it just displays the channel order wrong.

167

Multichannel Audio Clips

Put multichannel audio on multiple tracks

In earlier versions of Premiere, you needed to define the type of audio track before adding audio clips to the track. That process is no longer necessary.

Additionally, in the past, depending upon how a preference was set, a stereo clip would combine both channels into a single track. In fact, the current default preference is to match the file. So, a stereo clip would be placed on the Timeline with both channels of the clip in one track. A dual-channel mono clip would have one channel in one track and the second channel in a second track.

You can control this behavior for individual clips by using **Modify > Audio Channels**, or, right+click a clip in the Project Panel.

However, if you want to change this permanently, which makes more sense, go to **Preferences > Audio** and change the pop-up menu settings for Mono and Stereo.

- **Use File**. This adds an audio file to the Timeline to match the settings of the file. Mono clips as mono, stereo clips as stereo.

- **Mono**. This adds an audio file to the Timeline as a mono clip. Mono files put audio on a single track. Stereo files put their audio on two tracks.

- **Stereo**. This adds an audio file to the Timeline as a stereo clip (two channels in one track), even if only one track has audio in it.

- **5.1**. This adds an audio file to the Timeline as a 5.1 surround clip.

- **Adaptive**. This is an audio format designed for video games.

My preference is to set both Mono and Stereo clip preferences to **Mono**, which makes my audio editing life easier.

Intro to the Mixer

When you need more control than keyframes in a clip in the timeline

Hidden in plain sight in Premiere is a very capable mixer. To access the mixer:

- Select **Window > Audio Mixer** and select the sequence you want to mix,

- Or, click the Audio Mixer tab at the top of the Source Monitor,

- Or, select **Window > Workspace > Audio**,

- Or, type **Option+Shift+1 (Alt+Shift+1)**.

If you've never seen a mixer before, this panel can cause immediate terror.

However, it is important to note that a mixer is composed of channel strips—one for each track of audio in your sequence. Every channel strip is identical, so once you understand how one works, you've learned them all.

To return to the Source Monitor, click the tab at the top, or select **Window > Source Monitor** and select the sequence you want to view.

Note: The Mixer is especially helpful if you have an external control surface, which looks like a mixer except that it talks directly to the computer, that interfaces with Premiere. Control surfaces allow you to adjust multiple settings at once because you can get all ten fingers involved in the process.

Decoding the Channel Strip

Trust me, it really isn't as bad as it looks!

All track channel strips are identical. From the top:

Front left. Determines sound placement in a surround mix.

Master. Sends the channel output to the master output, or to submixes (more on this in a bit). Master is the default.

Pan knob. Pans the channel from full left to full right and everywhere in-between. This is called "placing the audio on the sonic stage (or sonic field)."

Yellow numbers at top. Displays the track pan setting. **–100** is left. **0** is center. **+100** is right.

Read. Turns on, or off, automatic keyframing during playback (more on this in a bit, as well).

M—S—R. Mute—Solo—Arm a track for recording.

Fader. A slider that adjusts the playback volume of a track.

Yellow numbers at bottom. Displays the track volume setting. 0.00 means the track is playing back at the level at which it was recorded.

Track label. Allows custom track names; double-click to change. (You can also right-click the track name and select **Rename**.)

Adjusting Audio Levels

Using the mixer allows greater precision.

The faders in Premiere Pro are very cool—because they give you a lot of information about the audio in your clip.

(Continued)

First, the simple stuff: to make a track louder, drag the fader up. To make it softer, drag it down.

The yellow numbers at the bottom show you the amount you are raising or lowering the volume of the track. The white numbers to the bottom right show the peak level of that track. Dynamic peak levels are the loudest level the clip has attained for the last couple of seconds.

The thin horizontal yellow bar at the top of the green column displays the peak level. The dark blue line in the middle of the clip displays the valley level—the softest level the clip has attained. Both of these indicators reset every few seconds.

Notice the two white scales? The one on the left shows how much you are altering the volume of the clip with the fader. The one on the right displays the current volume of that track. (The scale on the left is *relative*, the scale on the right is *absolute*.)

Note: How levels are displayed in the Mixer emulates the settings of the Audio Meters in the main editing workspace.

Fast Audio Reset

A quick way to reset an audio fader

The audio mixer was redesigned in Premiere CS6 to make it similar to the mixer in Audition. (And the benefit is that once you know how to use the mixer in one application, you already know how to use the mixer in the other.)

As you are dragging faders to set levels or pan, if you realize that your setting is just wrong, double-click the fader to reset it back to its default setting at Unity.

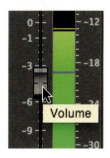

Automatically Recording Keyframes

This is a simple way to adjust audio levels in real time

The benefit to creating keyframes in the Timeline is that we can do it with the mouse, while the playhead is stopped, and it works fine for simple mixes.

The disadvantage is that you can't use the mouse to set keyframes during playback, which is a real bummer when your track count starts to rise.

What to do? Let Premiere Pro record the keyframes for you ... automatically. Here's how.

- Enlarge the Mixer to full screen (select the panel and press the Accent key) so you can see what you are doing.

- Click the pop-up menu at the top of the fader and set it to either **Write**, **Latch**, or **Touch**. (Personally, I use **Touch**. All three record keyframes the same way, but they don't *re*-record them the same way and I like how Touch handles re-recording.)

- Click the **Play** button at the bottom of the mixer to play the sequence from the top.

- Drag the fader up and down to adjust the level during playback so it sounds good to your ear. Repeat this process until you are happy with the sound of that track.

- Set the pop-up menu at the top to **Read**. This turns off recording keyframes, but plays the ones you've recorded. (If you want to have the track ignore all keyframes, set this pop-up to **Off**.)

- Play the sequence and admire your work.

Personally, I find this technique works the best when using a control surface.

So, Why Can't I See the Keyframes I Just Recorded?

Because the track keyframe display is turned off by default

By default, Premiere Pro shows clip keyframes. However, when you are recording keyframes using the Mixer, you are recording keyframes for the *track*. There are significant benefits to track keyframes—including the ability to have keyframe settings span more than one clip.

However, if you want to see the results of your mixing, not seeing the keyframes you just recorded is a bit, um, off-putting.

So, to display track keyframes, click the itty-bitty little icon in the track header that looks like a diamond—it is below and to the right of the speaker icon.

Switch the display from clip keyframes to track keyframes. This allows you to make changes to individual track keyframes, delete individual track keyframes, or delete all track keyframes.

Note: To delete a range of keyframes, select the Pen tool, drag a marquee around the keyframes you want to delete to select them, then press the **Delete** key.

Second Note: When track keyframes are displayed, clip-based operations on that track are turned off.

What Are Stems and Why Would You Create Them?

There are three common stems: dialog, effects, and music

A "stem" is a subset of your audio. There are three common stems: all dialog, all effects, and all music. Each stem is a stereo pair that can either be created by Premiere, or imported into Premiere from the final sound mix.

(Continued)

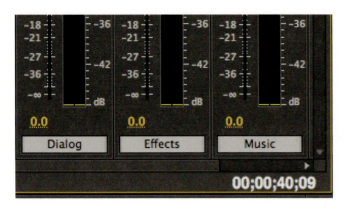

Because your master mix contains all your audio, fully mixed, why would anyone be interested in stems?

Here are two common reasons:

- For international versions, the translation company wants to be able to remove the English dialog and replace it with, say, Spanish, without changing the sound of the effects or music.

- For trailers, which completely reedit a project, the trailer editor wants access to dialog and effects, but not music. (The radical changes in the music would distract from the cut.) Then, when the trailer is reedited, the editor will replace the music so it sounds like it was recorded that way.

Note: Standard industry practice is that all stems are the same length, even if there is no audio for a large portion of the stem. This simplifies resyncing at any point in the future. Generally, the duration of a stem matches the duration of the program.

To be completely truthful, whereas Premiere Pro allows us to create submixes — coming up next—which are how we create stems, if my mix is getting that complicated, I'm moving it out of Premiere into Audition, which gives me greater control.

However, the Mixer in Premiere is a very powerful feature, so, as long as we are talking about audio, I want to mention submixes.

Note: Some editors call "stems" the source clips grouped by category and sent to an audio post house for final mixing. I've always known stems to be the finished mix of each of the audio elements in a category—dialog, effects, and music.

Creating a Submix—and Why

A submix allows you to group a portion of your audio into a single control

Submixes can be used to create stems, as we just discussed. However, I tend to use them more for reverb tracks, where I want to create a single reverb effect, but have it apply to clips on multiple tracks.

At some point, move the clips that you want to add reverb to separate tracks. For instance, I'll create a reverb track for a large space—like an aircraft hanger—and another reverb track for a smaller space—say a tunnel. This allows me to have different effects settings for the different tracks, without over-burdening the CPU with effects calculations.

Then, I route the audio from the source track to the appropriate reverb submix to achieve the effect I want.

To create a submix:

- Go to **Sequence > Add Tracks**.

- Select the number of submix tracks you want to create. In our example, we would create two submixes for reverb.

- Although it is not required, it's a good idea to name the submix; double-click the name at the bottom of the submix in the Mixer.

- Apply your effect.

- Go to the top of the channel strip that you want to send to the Reverb submix. Click the Master popup and select **Reverb**.

All tracks routed to the Reverb submix will have reverb.

Applying Effects in the Mixer

You can do it, but it's hidden

To apply an audio effect (FX) to a mixer channel, twirl down the small white triangle at the top left of the channel to which you want to apply the effect. (Audio effects are also called "filters" and the two words are used interchangeably.)

The white area divides into three areas—the top section is for effects.

Click the small gray triangle on the right edge of the white area—yes, I know, look at the screen shot—and a list of all the audio filters is displayed.

Select the filter you want to apply and it appears in a list at the top of the channel strip.

To change the filter settings, double-click the name of the filter at the top of the channel strip.

Note: The filter interface looks different in Premiere than it does in Audition. However, in general, filters that are named the same do the same, do the same things.

Sending Sequences to Audition

When you need more audio power, it's time to call on audition

Truthfully, when I start to think about submixes, sends, buses, and stems, its time to move out of Premiere Pro and into Audition. Audition is a full-featured, high-power audio repair, editing, and mixing application. I only discovered it recently, but I've become a big fan.

(*Continued*)

Because all Adobe applications support Dynamic Linking, the process of moving files from Premiere to Audition could not be easier:

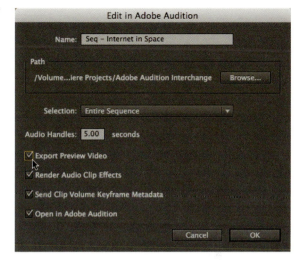

- In the Project panel, select the sequence you want to send to Audition.

- Then, either right-click and select **Edit in Adobe Audition > Sequence** or choose **Edit > Edit in Adobe Audition > Sequence**. (You can also send individual clips for repair—say to remove hum.)

- In the dialog that appears, give the file a name—it defaults to the name of the sequence. Most of the default settings are fine, but there are two I suggest you change:

- Set audio handles to between five and ten seconds. Just as handles are important in video editing, they are equally important in audio editing.

- Check "Export Preview Video." This generates a small video that can be viewed in Audition so that as you are mixing your audio, you can watch the video (this is called "Mix to Pix.")

The time it takes to create this movie totally depends upon the duration of your video project, but it won't take long. At which point, your project shows up in Audition ready to edit.

And Audition is what I want to talk about in the next chapter.

CHAPTER 8

Audition CS6

When you need more audio firepower than Premiere Pro can provide, it is time to turn to Audition. Audition began on Windows and developed a devoted following in radio broadcast production. It added a Mac version with the CS5.5 release. With the CS6 version, Adobe added a ton of new features and tied it even more tightly to Premiere Pro.

Sending Projects from Premiere Pro

Moving projects between applications could not be easier

When you send a file or project from Premiere Pro to Audition on the same system, Audition will open automatically, import the files, and properly configure a multitrack session based on what Premiere sent.

To export a sequence from Premiere Pro to send to Audition on a different system, use **File > Export > XML**. (You could also use OMF, but XML is better.) XML preserves stereo and 5.1 clips and tracks and doesn't force all clips to mono.

(Continued)

To open a file in Audition that was exported from Premiere Pro on a different system, use **File > Import**.

Note: Audition cannot import AAF files. Use either OMF or XML.

Importing Projects from Final Cut Pro

Importing is darn easy here, as well

To export a sequence from Final Cut Pro to Audition, first select the sequence in Final Cut's Browser, then select **File > Export > Audio to OMF**. This exports the audio files.

Then, use **File > Export > Using QuickTime Conversion** to create a small (320×240) movie to import into Audition so you can watch the picture while mixing.

Note: The default settings for this video export option are fine. Creating a small movie decreases the amount of work the CPU needs to use to play it back, thus allowing more power for audio in Audition.

Media Browser: A Fast Way to Review Files

This panel is a fast way to browse volumes, directories, or files

The Media Browser panel is new with the CS6 release. It allows you to quickly review the contents of volumes (hard disks), directories, and preview files before importing them. You can also use this panel to preview the properties of a file before importing.

One of the real time-saving features of the Media Browser panel is that you can drag-and-drop files from the Media Browser into the Editor, Files panel, Match or Batch panels, or any track in a Multitrack session.

(Continued)

The real benefit to using this panel is that you can quickly review files before wasting time importing and loading the wrong file.

Note: At the bottom right of the window is an auto-play toggle; a small speaker icon. When enabled, Audition automatically plays a file as soon as you select it.

The Difference Between Open and Import

It's not as big as you think

Hmmm ... which to choose: Open or Import?

Well, actually, it doesn't make a lot of difference, they both work the same. The only difference is that an audio file you "Open" is loaded into the Files panel and displayed in the Waveform Editor (for files) or Multitrack View (for sequences).

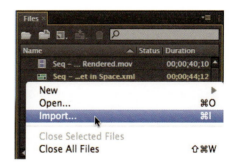

(Continued)

Imported files are loaded into the Files panel, but not displayed. (If you try to open a video file, Audition will object. Video files should always be imported.)

Note: Mac users can also drag and drop files into Audition from the Finder or drop them onto the Audition icon in the Dock.

Importing a Video File

Audition limits you to one video track, which can only hold one video clip

Audition is designed for audio, not video, editing. Consequently, it only provides one video track, which can contain exactly one video clip.

The process of importing video is exactly the same as importing an audio clip: **File > Import**. However, if you already have a video clip placed in a Multitrack session and attempt to add a second clip, Audition displays a warning dialog that it can only display one video clip at a time.

To load a video clip into a Multitrack session, drag it from the Files panel to anywhere in the Timeline. Audition will automatically place the video file on the correct track.

If you are exporting sequences from other applications for Audition, such as Final Cut Pro, be sure to create a single movie file for import into Audition along with the audio. As discussed earlier, use **File > Export > Using QuickTime Conversion**.

Note: You can drag and drop files directly from the Finder (or Explorer) into the Files panel.

Convert an Audio File Sample Rate

Audition requires audio sample rates to match throughout a sequence

The sample rate of a file determines the maximum frequency response of the audio. A sample rate of 48,000 (also called 48 kHz or cycles/second) supports a maximum frequency response of 24,000 cycles/second, which exceeds normal human hearing. However, there are several different audio sample rates that are used in video recording: 48 kHz, 44.1 kHz, and 32 kHz. Audition requires that all sample rates in the same session be the same.

If the sample rates don't match, Audition will automatically resample audio and create a new file when a file is imported into the current "Session" (Audition uses "Session" instead of "Sequence").

Convert Sample Type

Presets: (Default)

- (Default)
- 44.1 kHz, Stereo, 16–bit (Adaptive Noise Shaping)
- 44.1 kHz, Stereo, 16–bit (No Dither)
- 44.1 kHz, Stereo, 16–bit (Triangular Dither)
- Convert to 16–bit
- Convert to 24–bit
- Convert to 32–bit (IEEE Float)
- Convert to ITU 5.1
- Convert to Mono (Average)
- Convert to Stereo
- Resample to 32000 Hz
- Resample to 44100 Hz
- Resample to 47952 Hz
- Resample to 48000 Hz
- Resample to 48048 Hz
- Resample to 96000 Hz

Sample Rate Conversion
Sample Rate: 48000
▶ Advanced

Channels
Channels: Same as Source
▶ Advanced

Bit Depth
Bit Depth: 32
▶ Advanced

Cancel

However, sometimes you may want to convert these files manually—for example, when you want to replace the original file, or you need to tweak the settings beyond the defaults. When converting the sample rate, keep in mind that most sound cards only support certain sample rates, so its worthwhile to double-check what your card can handle.

To convert the sample rate of an audio file, open a file in the Waveform Editor and choose **Edit > Convert Sample Type**. From the preset menu, select the sample rate you want to convert into. Almost all video uses 48,000 samples per second, which makes this sample rate the best choice for video.

A fast way to access the Convert Sample Type dialog is to open a clip in the Waveform editor, then double-click the sample rate numbers displayed at the bottom of the window. This area is called the Status Bar.

(Continued)

Note: Audition's audio resampler is *much* better than Premiere Pro's. So if audio quality is really important, Adobe recommends opening the clip in the Audition Waveform Editor and changing the sample rate of the clip to match Premiere's sequence so that users don't have to use the resampler built into Premiere.

Tips on Converting Sample Rates

Just as with images, conversion risks a drop in quality

Here are some tips to keep in mind when changing sample rates using this dialog box:

- Both 44.1k and 48k sample rates support audio files with frequency responses that exceed normal human hearing. This makes them excellent for all types of audio recording.

- 32k sample rates are better for the spoken word than music. The benefit of this sample rate is smaller file sizes.

- Setting the **Quality** slider higher retains more high frequencies, but the conversion takes longer.

- Setting the **Quality** slider lower requires less processing time but reduces high frequencies.

- Use higher **Quality** values whenever you down-sample a high sample rate to a lower sample rate.

- When up-sampling audio, higher value settings for **Quality** will have little effect.

- For the best results, select **Pre/Post Filter** to prevent aliasing noise.

Note: Once you create a Multitrack session, you can't change sample rates for the session.

Share Markers Between Audition and Premiere

A new marker type makes this possible

There's a new marker type—called a Subclip range—that allows you to share Audition clip markers between Audition, Premiere Pro, and other applications in the Adobe Production Premium suite.

To create a marker to share between applications:

- Create a marker (type **M**).

- Right-click the marker and change it to a **Subclip**. The marker color turns blue.

- Right-click the marker, again, and change it to a **Range**. The marker displays a duration.

When you save the audio file and import it into Premiere, these markers are automatically converted into subclips that can be added into any sequence.

Note: You can change the marker type and duration in the Markers panel. You can convert a marker to a range by right-clicking the marker.

Sharing Preferences Between Systems

Easily standardize hardware preferences for multiple computers

If you have multiple computer systems editing audio, using common hardware and control surfaces, Audition makes it easy to standardize audio hardware, audio channel mapping, and control surface preferences between the different systems. These settings are stored in an XML file called: **MachineSpecificSettings.xml**—the location is listed below.

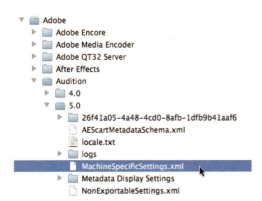

(Continued)

First, configure the preferences on one of your computers until you are happy. Then, copy the **MachineSpecificSettings.xml** file from your [Users folder] to:

- Win Vista/7/XP (64-bit): /Program Files (x86)/Common Files/Adobe/ Audition/5.0/

- Win Vista/7/XP (32-bit): /Program Files/Common Files/Adobe/ Audition/5.0

- Mac OS X: /Library/Preferences/Adobe/Audition/5.0/

Next, go to the Audio Hardware preferences page and ensure **Use Machine-specific device defaults** is selected. Finally, restart Audition.

When the XML file is found in the shared location *and* this preference option is checked, the hardware options specified will override any user profile preferences simplifying moving files and projects between workstations.

Copy this file on all systems that you want to share settings.

Getting Touchy-Feely with Your Audio

Mac trackpad gestures are now supported

The CS6 version of Audition now supports Pinch to Zoom and Rotate gestures when using a Mac with a touchpad.

Pinch to Zoom zooms in or out of the selected panel (where appropriate) and Rotate scrubs through the audio.

Note: Gesture support is not available on Windows.

To Hear, or Not To Hear

That is the new option

In past versions of Audition, when two clips overlapped, Audition would automatically create a cross-fade. However, sometimes you want the overlapping clip to block what was below it and you just don't have time to get everything trimmed properly. (This blocking behavior is the way video editing has always worked, but this is a new concept to audio.)

Now, there's a preference setting that allows you to toggle between playing overlapping clips with a cross-fade, or have the clip on top block the clip under it. Go to **Audition > Preferences > Multitrack**.

- **Automatically crossfade overlapping clips**. When checked, Audition cross-fades two overlapped clips; this is the default setting. When not checked, the audio cuts from one clip to the other, based on which clip is on top.

- **Play overlapped portions of clips**. When checked, Audition plays both clips during the overlap. When not checked, only the top clip will play.

- There are also new keyboard and menu options that allow you to change the stacking order of overlapped clips. For example, select **Clip > Send to Back** to send the selected clip to the back. Or, right-mouse-click a clip and select **Send to Back**.

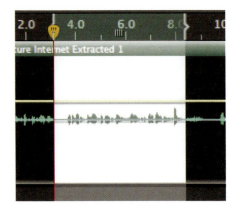

Selecting Regions

The time selection tool is a great way to select a portion of a clip

The Time Selection tool (**T**) is a great way to select a portion of a clip.

- Select the tool and drag inside a clip to select a region.

- To select the same region across multiple clips, either drag across all tracks, or select the first region, then **Command (Control)+click** to select matching regions on other tracks.

- To adjust the width of the region, grab either edge with the Time Selection tool and drag.

- To deselect the region, switch to the Move tool (**V**), and click anywhere outside the selected area.

Note: This is a very powerful, and flexible, tool—as you'll see in the next several tips.

Trim to Selection

A old trimming technique reappears with a new name

Audition 3, an earlier Windows-only version, had the ability to trim a clip to match the selection range. That feature reappeared with Audition CS6, but with a new name.

Use the Time Selection tool (**T**) and select a clip range in either the Timeline or Waveform Editor. Choose **Clip > Trim to Time Selection**. Poof!

Note: As with any time selection, you can use this to span multiple clips in the Multitrack Timeline.

Copy a Portion of a Clip

A fast way to copy a clip range

If you are in the Multitrack editor and need to copy a portion of a clip, but don't want to cut the clip, use the Time Selection tool (**T**) to select the range you want to copy.

Then, press **Option** and drag the title header at the top of the selected portion of the clip (the part that contains the clip name) to a new location.

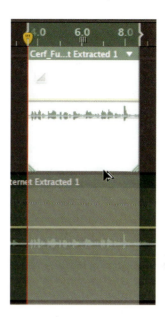

Create a Test Case

I love this feature—test an edit before making an edit!

There's a small, unassuming button in Audition CS6 that allows you to hear what removing a section of audio will sound like *before* you actually remove it. It's called Skip Selection.

- Start by clicking the **Skip Selection** button in the transport section.

- Next, using the Time Selection tool, select the range you are thinking of removing in the Timeline. Press **Play**.

The playhead backs up the preroll duration, plays and skips the selected range, and plays for the postroll duration. This is a great way to test an edit before you make it.

If the edit doesn't sound right, adjust the Time Selection by dragging one of the vertical edges.

Note: Here's a really fast way to change the preroll duration: just move the playhead to where you want the preroll to start. That sets the preroll; the postroll matches that duration. Audition will use this duration in the future until you change it.

Trained for Clip Spotting

Precisely position clips using the properties panel

Have you ever wanted to have a clip start precisely at a specific time in the Timeline? Or end at a precise moment? Or run for a specific amount of time? Now you can, here's how.

● Select a clip in the Multitrack Timeline.

● Open the Properties panel.

● Enter any combination of starting or ending times, or the duration you want.

The lower half of the Properties window allows additional settings to be changed for the clip.

Note: You can also change any of these values by scrubbing directly on the number values.

Select Clips from Playhead to End

A quick way to select a bunch of clips on a track

Here's a fast way to select a group of clips—specifically, from the current position of the playhead to the end of the session.

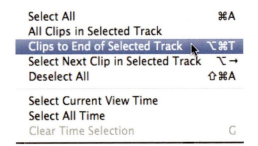

● Put your playhead where you want the selection to start.

● Select a clip in the track that contains the clips you want to select.

● Choose **Edit > Select > Select Clips to End of Track**, or type **Option+Command+T** (**Alt+Control+T**).

If you first select clips on multiple tracks, you can extend the number of tracks included in the selection.

190

(Continued)

Once you have the clips selected, you can move or delete them as a group, without converting them into a group.

Note: This only selects whole clips. You can't use this to select a portion of a clip.

Lock Your Clips

Lock in time prevents clips from shifting horizontal position

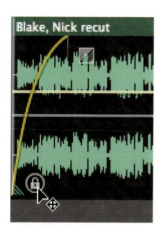

This is a very important technique for video editors who are mixing sync sound in Audition. Although we can lock tracks to prevent changes, that makes trimming and adding fades really awkward. What we want is to allow a clip to move between tracks, but not shift from side to side, which would knock it out of sync. A perfect example of this is audio that is imported from Premiere and is synced to video.

Piece of cake. Right-click the clip and select **Lock in Time**. This locks the clip horizontally, but allows you to move it vertically. The small circle indicator in the low left corner of the clip indicates that it is locked in time.

Note: You can also lock a clip in time using the Properties menu.

Fast Tip for a Fast Edit

Need to edit a file FAST? Here's how …

When speed is critical, double-click a file name in the Media Browser panel. Audition CS6 instantly opens it in the Waveform editor panel for fast editing.

You don't even need to import it first!

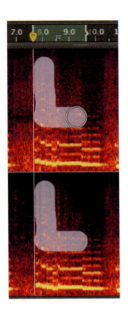

Audio, Heal Thyself!

A keyboard shortcut to control healing

When working with audio in the frequency spectral display, the ability to remove problem audio using the healing brush approaches the magical.

- Open a clip in the Waveform editor.

- Display the spectral view (**Shift+D**).

- Select the Spot Healing Brush tool (**B**).

- Drag the healing brush over a pop, click, squeal, or burbling cell phone in the spectral view and—poof!—it's gone.

New with the CS6 version is the ability to restrict the direction of movement when using the Healing Brush. Hold the **Shift** key down and you'll only be able to drag the brush either horizontally or vertically.

Yup, It's Too Loud

Audition can test your files for being too loud

Many years of experience have taught me that it is far better to discover problems in your audio *before* sending it to the client. And the Amplitude Statistics window makes that really easy.

In fact, I created a keyboard shortcut for it to make this even more accessible:

- Open the clip, or mixdown, you want to test into the Waveform editor. (Once a mixdown is complete, it always shows up in the File Browser, which makes it easy to access.)

- Select **Window > Amplitude Statistics**.

(Continued)

- Click the **Scan** button in the lower left corner to have it calculate your levels. (This will take a few seconds, depending on the length of your session.)

There are three settings I make a point to review before releasing my audio:

- **Peak amplitude**. For my mixes, I like keeping this close to −3 dB.

- **Possibly Clipped Samples**. I always want this to be zero.

- **Total RMS Amplitude**. I want this to be between −20 and −23.

New regulations in Europe require monitoring mix levels for broadcast so that they are not too loud, according to regulations called ITU-R BS.1770-2. At the bottom of this window, it shows a value next to ITU-R BS.1770-2 Loudness. This is measured in LUFS (sometimes called LKFS). For EBU work, this needs to be close to −23.

Note: You can copy the loudness value to the clipboard using the **Copy All** button.

A Fast Way to Merge Clips

Open append easily combines clips

Let's say you have a file open in the Waveform Editor and you want to add another file to it. Select **File > Open Append > To Current** and the new file is added to the end of the file currently displayed in the Waveform Editor.

Or, say you have a bunch of files on your hard disk that you want to bundle together into a single new file, select **File > Open Append > to New**. This collects all the files into a single audio file and adds markers to the new clip indicating the name and location of each of the appended files.

Move Your Markers

Drag and drop markers from the markers panel to your session

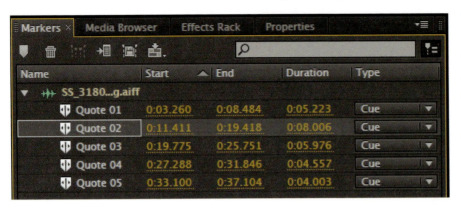

When you are in the Markers panel, you can now drag and drop marker ranges from individual clips directly onto a Multitrack session. I find this a very helpful technique for interviews. I flag a quote with a marker range, then drag that marker into my edit where I need to insert the quote. (For this to work, the marker must include an audio range.)

- Click the button in the top right corner of the Markers panel to toggle either viewing just markers in the active document or all markers for all files.

- When viewing markers for all files, you can drag and drop marker ranges into any Multitrack session to create new clips using those ranges.

- Double-click any marker in the Markers panel to open its associated timeline and make it the active document.

- When viewing all markers, you can only edit the data stored in a marker for a session or clip that is currently displayed in either the Multitrack Timeline or the Waveform editor.

Note: New with CS6, when you are in the Markers panel, you are able to view and search through all the markers in all open assets.

Mark CD Tracks

New CD track markers for creating music CDs

There are new CD Track markers in Audition that allow you to specify exactly where the tracks change when burning a session to a CD. This allows you to put all your final CD tracks into one session and separate them using CD Track markers to simplify creating your CD. The keyboard shortcut is **Shift+M**.

A clip, or session, must be displayed in either the Multitrack or Waveform views in order to change or delete markers.

Note: You can easily change marker types in the Markers panel, and you can use **Preferences > Appearance** to change the color of CD Track markers.

A Fast Way to Burn a CD Master

Here's a fast way to create an audio CD using marker ranges

A good reason to use Open Append is when you want to burn a quick CD with all your music tracks on it. Try this:

- **File > Open Append > To New**

- Choose the files you want to open and append into a new single file.

- Once the file opens and all of the audio assets are appended (surrounded by markers), open the Markers panel.

- Select all Markers in the panel, right-click and change the type to **CD Track**.

- Go to **File > Export > Burn Audio to CD**

This burns a CD with each marker range created as a new track on the CD.

(Continued)

Note: A clip, or session, must be displayed in either the Multitrack or Waveform views in order to change or delete markers.

Save Time, Create Templates

Create a session template for tasks that you do over and over

A session template is a special kind of Multitrack session, where you configure all your settings first, then save it as a template. This can save a ton of time when you are doing the same kind of recording over and over again.

To create a template, create a new Multitrack session and configure as you see fit. To save it as a template, select **File > Export > Session as Template**.

To create a new Multitrack session using a template, select **File > New > Multitrack Session**. Then, from the drop-down dialog in the dialog, select the saved template you want to use.

Unless you specify a specific location for a template, Audition stores templates here:

- **Mac**: \Users\Shared\Adobe\Audition\5.0\Session Templates\

- **Windows XP**: \Documents and Settings\All Users\Documents\Adobe\ Audition\5.0\Session Templates\

- **Windows Vista**: \Users\Public\Public Documents\Adobe\Audition\5.0\ Session Templates\

- **Windows 7**: \Users\Public\Public Documents\Adobe\Audition\5.0\ Session Templates\

196

(Continued)

You can change this location by going to **Preferences > Media & Disk Cache** and changing the Session Templates location.

Align Speech Automatically

A fast, automatic way to align two clips for ADR

Here's the scenario: your source clip was recorded on set, but there was noise. You need to go back into the audio studio and re-record that dialog. This is the time-consuming process of ADR (Automatic Dialog Replacement).

The problem isn't the recording or your actors, it's getting the new audio to sync with the old audio and action. Audition CS6 provides a fast way to align the new clip with the old clip.

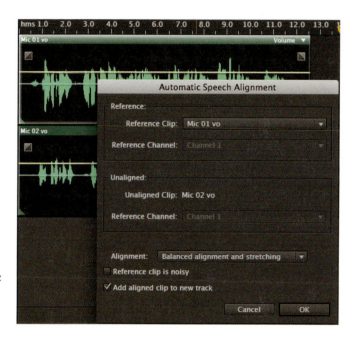

- Place the original source audio clip in Track 1.

- Place the new audio into Track 2, or you can record the new audio directly into Track 2.

- Select both clips and choose **Clip > Automatic Speech Alignment** (or right click both clips and choose **Automatic Speech Alignment**).

- In the dialog that appears, specify the reference clip and the new, or unaligned, clip. You can also choose a specific channel to reference from each clip.

Audition then creates a new aligned clip and puts it on a new track. (You also have the option to only have the new file added to the Files panel and not a new track.)

While this technique can be used for any type of audio, it will sound the best when you use it for clips that only contain speech.

Like Sand Drifting Through an Hourglass

Add a metronome to your session

In Audition CS6, we can now add a metronome to a Multitrack session. A button to the left of the top time ruler toggles the metronome track.

A metronome track acts exactly like a regular track—the only difference being that clips cannot be placed on it and audio cannot be routed to it. What a metronome track does is produce a metronome pulse at the tempo of your session. (You can modify these settings in the Properties panel, provided that no clips are edited into the session.)

Because the metronome is part of a normal audio track, its output can be routed as needed, Sends can be used to route to multiple outputs, and it can be muted, soloed, and its volume and pan adjusted.

In fact, if you select **Multitrack > Metronome**, you'll see a variety of different beat patterns and sound sets; some of which are quite wild.

Note: The metronome tempo should match your session start time, as set in the session properties. Also, you can set a keyboard shortcut, or MIDI input, to toggle the metronome on or off.

Generating Tone

Create a tone and see what it looks like

Choose **Effects > Generate Tones** to create a steady tone. These are frequently used for testing gear and signal paths.

- Select **Effects > Generate Tones**.

- Specify the type of clip. (**48k** sample rate, **32-bit depth** is a good choice.)

(Continued)

- Use **Default** to create a standard, 440-cycle tone. Adjust the frequency to change pitch.

This window allows you to preview the tone and adjust settings.

Note: Check out the presets for some very intriguing possibilities. I laughed out loud with **Note Deep**.

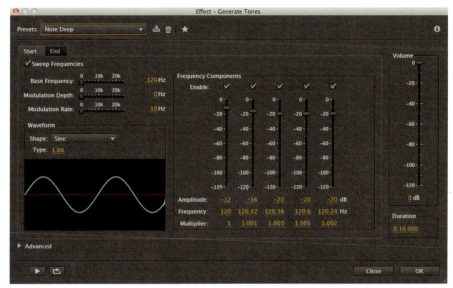

Create a Group

Groups allow you to lock multiple clips together

Grouping clips allows you to treat separate clips as if they are a single clip. This often makes large projects much more manageable, and helps avoid making mistakes.

To group clips:

- Select the clips you want to group

Do one of the following:

- Type **Command (Control)+G**

- Select **Clip > Group > Group Clips**

- Right-click within the selected clips and select: **Group > Group clips**

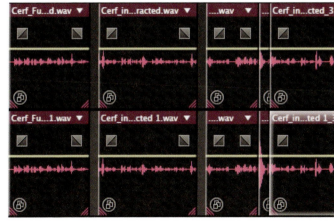

Clips that are grouped change color and show a group icon in the lower-left corner of each clip in the group.

First Among Equals

Focus allows you to work with a clip contained in a group

Grouping clips allows you to treat a collection of audio clips as though they were a single clip. However, sometimes, it would be really helpful to modify a clip that's locked in a group. For instance, to apply or modify an effect filter for a single clip.

With the CS6 release, you can now focus a clip—click it and see a slight glow surround the clip. This focus state allows you to add, modify, or delete filters applied to the clip in the Effects rack without breaking the group.

Note: You can't delete or move the focused clip separately while it is still attached to a group.

Suspending Groups

Suspending temporarily ungroups a group

Here's another new group feature—Suspending. Sometimes, you need to work with individual clips contained in a group. Normally, you can't; that's why you created the group in the first place.

However, you can suspend group behavior without destroying the group. Think of this as a Pause switch. Pause the group, move clips around, add filters, trim clips, then unpause it to return to the group.

To work this magic, do *one* of the following:

- **Shift+Command+G (Shift+Control+G)**.
- Select **Clip > Groups > Suspend Groups**.
- Right-click within the group and select **Groups > Suspend Groups**.

(*Continued*)

To unsuspend a group, do one of the above three steps again.

Note: Suspended groups retain their group color, but the icon in the lower left corner changes shape.

A New Audio Envelope

Use envelopes to control both gain and fades

New with Audition CS6 is the Gain Envelope. This allows you to change the gain of a clip up to +15 dB. Generally, you shape the gain for a clip or a track using keyframes. What's especially nice about this feature is that as you drag keyframes, a small popup display shows the gain change in both dB and percentage.

The old Amplitude envelope was renamed to Fade Envelope, because that's a better description of what it does—provide precise control over complex fades at the end of a clip.

Lock Your Keyframes

Locking keyframes prevents accidentally altering a mix

Just picture it: you've spent the last hour tweaking the keyframes for a track so it sounds perfect. Then, when you thought you selected the track just below it and started resetting keyframes, you discover you totally hosed the track you just finished.

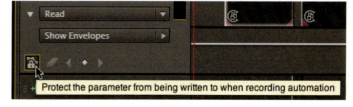

After you finish screaming at the computer, what do you do? You prevent accidentally changing keyframes by locking an envelope. This process is called **Safe During Write**.

(Continued)

To lock the track keyframes in an envelope in Multitrack view:

● Expand the Track Header so you can see the Read pop-up menu.

● Twirl down the triangle next to the Read pop-up menu.

● Click the little lock icon in the track header. It's just to the left of the Eraser. This prevents making changes to keyframes in that track.

Tandem Keyframes

Clip keyframes and track keyframes work together

In Audition, you can apply keyframes both to the track and clips contained inside that track. When you do, both are active, which is not the same behavior as Premiere Pro.

Snap Back to 0

A fast way to reset envelopes

You can quickly reset the track pan, clip pan, and volume envelopes to **0** using snapping. In fact, snapping is now the default. As you drag an envelope and it gets within about 5 pixels of 0 dB, the line snaps into the 0 dB position.

This is great, except when you don't want it. To override snapping, press **Command (Control)** while dragging an envelope.

Hear a Mono Mix of your Project

With the click of a button you can switch between stereo and mono

Ever wonder what this button does in the Master track at the bottom of the Multitrack window? It's a temporary switch that allows you to hear your stereo mix in mono. Press it, and you hear mono. Let go and the system reverts to stereo.

This is really useful when you are creating a mix that will be heard in stereo in some situations and mono in others. This allows you to check for phase cancellation or other weirdness when converting stereo to mono.

(By the way, this button only appears on stereo tracks. Mono tracks don't need it.)

Note: This feature is designed for Audio General Rule #1: If you check something *before* release, there's never a problem. When you fail to check, chaos ensues.

Can't Have Too Many Plug-Ins

And now, you can get them organized

Audition has long been able to work with plug-ins, using an audio format called VST. Now, you can organize all your third-party plug-ins by:

- Vendor
- Category
- Vendor, then Category
- Category, the Vendor
- None

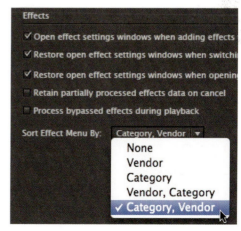

You set this up using **Preferences > Effects > Sort Effect Menu By**.

Note: This is a display-only function and doesn't change how effects are applied or processed.

Set Side-Chain Input

Effects Can Now Be Side-Chained

Side-chaining allows one effect to alter another effect

Side-chaining allows the output of a track to control an effect. For example, the output of a kick drum track can control a gain filter applied to a bass guitar track. This would have the result of making the kick drum and bass guitar sound more in sync by amplifying the bass guitar at the instant the kick is heard.

Another good example is automatically ducking the music when a voice over starts.

Here's how this works:

- Insert an effect capable of side chain control—say, Dynamics Processing—on the desired track. Set the effect to key from a Side-Chain signal, this setting will vary from effect to effect.

- In the standard effects interface, press the **Set Side-Chain Input** button at the top of the effect interface and select the desired Side-Chain input (Mono, Stereo, or 5.1; usually the same as the control track).

- In the effects interface, press the **Channel Map Editor** button—it is just to the right of the side-chain button—and set the desired side chain routing to the effect input (this should happen automatically).

- In the Side-Chain control track, use one of sixteen available Sends to route audio control information to the input of the Side-Chain effect via **Side-Chain > Effect Name** (Track Name—Slot name) ...

- The Side-Chain Send will automatically be set to 0 dB in Prefader mode. This can be changed if needed.

- Use the standard send controls to set the pan and level of the side chain control signal to the effect.

204

(Continued)

This will send the control audio from the send of the track and route it into the Side-Chain key input of the selected effect. Use this to let one audio signal control an effect on another track.

Channel Your Effects

See the internal routing of your effects

Want to see the internal routing of an effect? Open the effect and, in the top right corner, press the **Channel Map Editor** button.

This shows the input (on the left) and output (on the right) of the effect and illustrates the signal flow between them. You can rearrange the signal flow, or select which channels to process with the effect.

You can also use this to rearrange the internal routing of an audio file by inserting an effect into the audio chain.

Changing Pitch

There are two ways to change the pitch of a clip

There are two ways to change the pitch of a clip: Manual and Automatic.

The automatic pitch correction is new with the CS6 release and is a real-time effect. Select a clip and choose **Effects > Pitch and Time > Automatic Pitch Correction**. In the dialog window, you can select the scale and key you want the clip to match, as well as adjust the speed and degree of pitch change.

This automatic effect is available in both Multitrack and Waveform views.

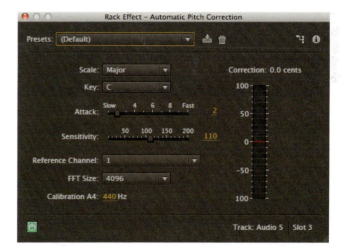

(Continued)

A quick note: slow attacks (that is, the start of the effect) sound more natural, but won't fix fast pitch changes. Fast attacks solve that problem but sound more mechanical and auto-tuney. In a Multitrack session, this effect is the best option when applied to individual clips that need a quick adjustment.

When you want to get more precise, use a manual pitch change. Open a clip in the Waveform Editor, then select: **Effects > Time and Pitch > Manual Pitch Correction**. The best way to use this is to display the spectral view (**Shift+D**). After a few seconds, a blue line describing the pitch is superimposed over the frequency display. Just as with volume envelopes, adjust the shape of this envelope to adjust the pitch of the file.

Note: It is considered bad form to apply both automatic and manual correction to the same clip. Just pick one.

The Pitch Profile Button

This button allows you to preview pitch changes

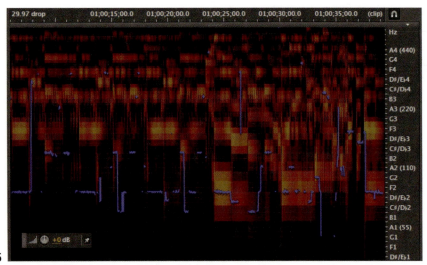

Normally, you use the spectral view to preview pitch changes. However, when you click the **Pitch Profile** Button, near the Spectral Frequency Display button, you can view the pitch profile—that is, a line that displays how the pitch is changing in a clip—as a side-by-side option with the waveform display.

When you use this button, pitch is displayed as blue-lines. This is read-only mode; you can't make changes to the pitch line. If you need to make changes, open the Manual Pitch Correction effect using **Effects > Time and Pitch > Manual Pitch Correction**.

206

Create A Favorite Effect

Save your customized settings as a favorite

You've created this absolutely killer combination of great effects in the Effects Rack. Now you can save it as a Favorite so that you can reuse it in a heartbeat. (Well, maybe two heartbeats.)

Load and configure effects in the Effects Rack until you're happy with the sound. Then, click the **Star** icon at the top of the Rack panel to save your settings as a Favorite.

Access your favorites from the Presets pop-up menu at the top of the Effects Rack.

SOOO Close ... But Not Quite

That darn recording is three-quarters of a second too long

You created the perfect recording—technically flawless and the actor's reading was amazing ... except, its just three-quarters of a second too long.

Drat!

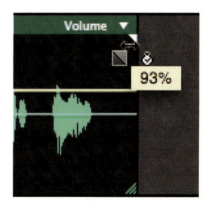

Now you can fix it by stretching your clip—either longer or shorter. This changes the duration of the clip, without changing the pitch. (Within reason; there's no free lunch.)

Here's how:

● Select the clip.

● Right+click and choose **Stretch > Stretch Mode > Real-Time**. (If you don't do this, you'll simply trim the end of the clip.) You can also turn stretching on from the Properties panel.

207

(*Continued*)

- Once this menu choice is enabled, drag the small triangle near the top right corner of the clip and stretch it to the length you need. The yellow tool-tip shows how much you are altering the clip.

Note: You can also use this same technique for a group of clips.

Audition Shortcuts

Faster ways to do common stuff

Here are some keyboard shortcuts that I use a lot for common tasks.

Shortcut	What It Does
Command (Control)+scroll wheel	Zoom in and out of Waveform editor or Multitrack Timeline
Shift+Delete	Delete selected segment and close gap in Multitrack View
Option (Alt) + Delete	Delete selected slice and close gap in Multitrack View
Command (Control) + left arrow	Jump to previous edit point in Multitrack View
Command (Control) + right arrow	Jump to next edit point in Multitrack View

A Fast Way to Add a Keyboard Shortcut

Double-click your way to faster editing with shortcuts

Need to create a custom keyboard shortcut in a hurry? Careful; Adobe moved the location of the Keyboard Shortcuts menu:

- Choose **Edit > Keyboard Shortcuts.**

- Scroll down until you find the menu option to which you want to add a keyboard shortcut.

- Double-click in the empty Shortcut column and enter your shortcut.

- Click **Save**.

Finding Duplicate Shortcuts

A quick way to track down duplicate keystrokes

You just added a new keyboard shortcut, only to see a warning that some other menu item is using the same shortcut; and that it has just been deleted.

Drat! That may not have been wise.

To hunt down that duplicate critter, click the **Go To Conflict** button. This quickly scrolls the list to display the offending shortcut. This allows you to either change it to a different key, or simply remove it.

Print Your Keyboard Shortcuts

Too cool for school—print your shortcut cheat sheet

Want a list of all the keyboard shortcuts in Audition all formatted to print? Couldn't be easier:

- Select **Edit > Keyboard Shortcuts**.

- Click **Copy to Clipboard**. This button copies all your shortcuts to the clipboard.

- Open the spreadsheet program of your choice and paste.

Voilà! Instant cheat sheet.

Mixdown Options

Where you select to create a mixdown makes a difference

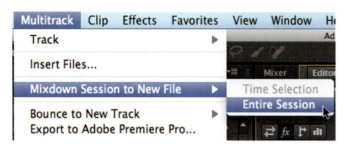

The Mixdown commands, found under both the File and Multitrack menus, don't have shortcuts assigned by default, mainly because there are so many options, Adobe wanted to give you the option to pick the option that works the best for you, then create your own shortcut for it.

However, *where* you select Mixdown makes a difference in *what* happens next.

When you select **Multitrack > Mixdown Session to New File > Entire Session**, the mixdown occurs and the resulting file opens in the Waveform Editor. This allows you to check it for levels, perform audio repairs, and so on.

Note: This mixes the session, but doesn't save it. You **must** save the file from the Waveform Editor.

When you select **File > Export > Multitrack Mixdown > Entire Session**, additional export settings become available, and your Multitrack session remains active while the file is saved in the background. When the mixdown is complete, the final file is displayed in the Files panel so you can load it into the Waveform editor to check levels.

So, if you are done with the file and want to create and save your mix the fastest way possible, select **File > Export > Multitrack Mixdown >Entire Session**.

Sending Mixdowns back to Premiere

Here's how to get your final mix back to Premiere—fast!

Just as we can send files from Premiere to Audition quickly, we can get them back to Premiere equally quickly.

(Continued)

Open your completed session into the Multitrack view.

Select **Multitrack > Export to Adobe Premiere Pro.**

In the dialog, give your final mix a name. Then, if you want to export a stereo mix for your project, check **Mixdown Session to > Stereo**. (By default, Audition creates stems.)

Also, make sure **Open in Adobe Premiere Pro** is checked.

Audition creates the mix, saves the file, opens Premiere Pro, and puts the file on the track you specify in the project.

This is both fast and simple.

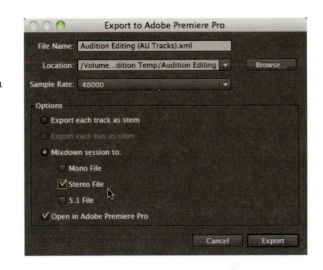

Exporting Mixdowns to Final Cut Pro

No automatic link but very fast, nonetheless

The easiest way to get audio out of Audition is to select **File > Export > Multitrack Mixdown >Entire Session**.

In the dialog that appears, give the file a name and location. In general, WAV format is the fastest and with excellent quality; use a 48kHz sample rate and 16-bit depth.

Click **OK** to generate the mix. This creates a master mix of the entire project.

Open FCP and import the file. Drag it from the Final Cut Browser to the Timeline and be sure it starts at the very beginning of the Timeline so it stays in sync with the video clips in your FCP project.

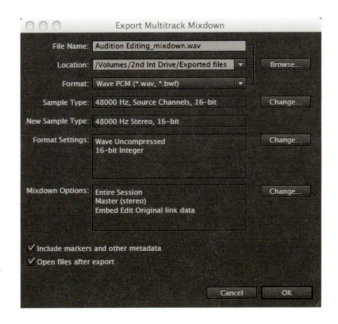

Saving Files From the Waveform Editor

Send files to audition for repair; now get them back quickly

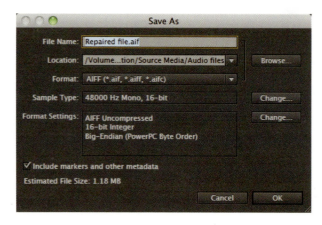

You sent a file to the Waveform editor for repair, say, to remove some hum.

Now, you need to get it back. The easiest way to do this is select: **File > Save As**.

Give the file a name and location, make sure it is either AIF or WAV, with a 48k sample rate and 16-bit depth.

Click **OK**.

Note: Audition is optimized to export WAV files. I recommend it when you are decided what audio format to use.

C H A P T E R 9

Premiere Pro—Transitions, Titles, and Effects

Whereas we tell stories with editing and spark the imagination with audio, we capture the eye with transitions, titles, and effects. This chapter looks at how to speed the process of creating visual effects. The only problem with this chapter is that it is just too short. Effects can fill an entire book by itself. So here we will just skim the highlights.

Let's start by looking at transitions.

Default Video or Audio Transitions

Here's a fast way to create an audio or video transition

You can add the default *video* transition between clips in a video track by typing **Command+D** (Mac OS) or **Ctrl+D** (Windows)

You can add the default *audio* transition between two clips in an audio track by pressing **Command+Shift+D** or, for Windows, **Ctrl+Shift+D**.

Setting the Duration of the Default Transition

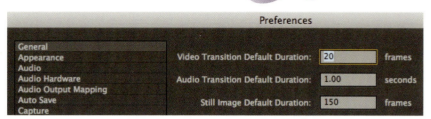

The default video transition is 30 frames. The default audio transition is one second. However, these are easy to change in Preferences. (In fact, I prefer a shorter dissolve for my default video transition and I use so many different audio transition lengths that I leave the default unchanged.).

To set the default transition duration in CS6:

- Go to **Premiere Pro > Preferences > General** (Mac OS)—or—**Edit > Preferences > General** (Windows).

- Change the value for the Video Transition Default Duration or Audio Transition Default Duration.

- Click **OK**.

Delete a Transition

It's all about the icon

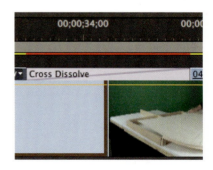

To delete a transition, click the transition icon in the top corner of a clip and press **Delete**.

The only reason I mention this is that when you are zoomed out on the Timeline, those transition icons can be very hard to see, so I wanted to tell you where to look.

Replace a Transition

Experimenting with different looks is easy

To swap one transition for another, drag the new video or audio transition from the Effects panel onto the existing transition in the sequence.

When you replace a transition, the alignment and duration are preserved. However, this discards any custom settings for the old transition and replaces it with the default settings for the new transition.

Customizing a Transition

Virtually every transition can be tweaked

While almost all transitions can be customized, the customization options vary from one transition to another. To open the Effect Controls panel, double-click the transition in the Timeline.

The top portion of this panel is similar for all transitions and allows you to:

- Preview a transition (click the small, white, right-pointing triangle).

- Change the duration (enter a new Duration value).

- Change the alignment of where the transition starts or ends.

- Adjust whether a transition completes, or if it stops part-way through the transition.

- Ripple or roll the edit point under the transition.

(Continued)

The bottom portion of this panel varies by transition. In this screen shot, you can add and modify the border between two images, change the direction of the transition, and adjust anti-aliasing; this last smooths clip edges which are not quite vertical or not quite horizontal.

Trim the Edit Under a Transition

Adjusting the edit point is easy using the effect controls panel

In the top right corner of the Effect Controls panel are small icons that illustrate the transition and the clips underneath it. The top clip represents the out-going clip, the bottom clip represents the in-coming clip, and the purple area in the middle represents the duration of the transition.

To ripple trim a clip under the transition, click the edge between the light blue (the clip in the timeline) and the dark blue (the handles, or extra video at the end of a clip), and drag. The edit point in the Timeline is automatically adjusted.

To roll trim the edit point between two clips, grab the purple box between the two clips and drag left or right.

To change the duration of a transition, and to create asymmetric transitions which are not centered on an edit point (which is very cool!), drag the edge of the purple box between the two clips.

Change Where a Transition Ends

Transitions don't have to end at the end, they can end in the middle

If you look really carefully under the large icons indicating each side of a transition in the Effect Controls panel, you'll see two dark sliders. These allow you to adjust whether a transition flows all the way from one clip to the next,

(Continued)

or stops in the middle. (By the way, if you want to see the actual source images in this preview, check the **Show Actual Sources** checkbox, just below these two icons.)

Why would you want to adjust where a transition ends? Let's say you want a transition to wipe into a split screen. Adjusting where a transition ends allows you to create this effect. Otherwise, the transition would wipe all the way through to the second clip, then cut to the effect.

Totally not the same thing.

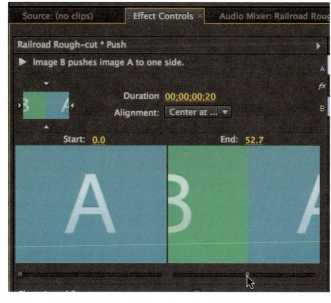

Transitions Can Be Single-Sided

You can create a transition that spans only one clip

Transitions typically have two sides—between the end of the out-going clip and the start of the in-coming clip. However, you can create a transition that affects only the beginning or end of a single clip—even when two clips touch. This is called a single-sided transition.

Single-sided transitions allow more control over how clips transition. Here, for instance, the first clip is fading to black using a Cross-fade, while the second clip slides in with a Push slide.

You can tell the difference, if your eyesight is good, between these two types of transitions by looking in the Timeline panel or the Effect Controls panel. A double-sided transition has a dark diagonal line through it, while a single-sided transition is split diagonally with one half dark and one half light.

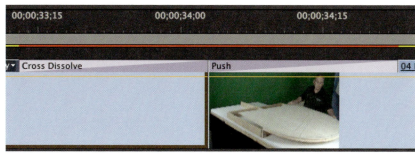

(Continued)

To create a single-sided transition:

- Drag a transition from the Effects panel to the edge of the clip to which you want to apply the transition.

- Press the **Command** (Mac) or **Control** (Windows) key before letting go of the mouse.

- Release the mouse when the appropriate edge—the end of the out-going clip or the start of the in-coming clip—highlights.

Note: Single-sided transitions fade to and from a transparent state, not to and from black. This means you can use this technique for B-roll clips.

Extra Credit: To place a transition at the end of a clip that is not touching another clip, drag and drop the transition. Don't use the modifier key. The transition automatically becomes single-sided.

Fade to Black. Really.

A cross-fade transition doesn't fade to black

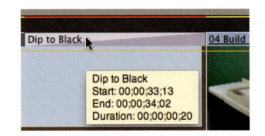

With one exception, all transitions fade to transparency, not black. Most of the time, this isn't a problem, but you need to understand the difference.

Whatever is below the transition in the Timeline panel appears in the transparent portion of the transition (the part of a transition where you don't see the existing clip). If the clip is on Video 1 or has no clips beneath it, the transparent portions display black and will output black when you export. If the clip is on a track above another clip, the lower clip shows through the transition.

When you want to fade to black between clips, you have two choices:

- Use the **Dip To Black** dissolve. Dip To Black doesn't reveal any underlying clips; it always fades to solid, non-transparent black.

(Continued)

- Add a title clip filled with black, to create a black clip, either next to, or under, the transition.

Keep in mind that because Dip to Black expects to fade out one clip, then fade in another, the duration of this effect is always half as long as its duration. So, a 30 frame Dip to Black transition will fade the first clip in 15 frames.

Create a Title

Why use premiere pro to create a title? Because it is easy!

Yes, you can create titles in Photoshop. You can even animate titles in After Effects. So, I already hear you asking: "Why create a title in Premiere Pro when we have After Effects?" And the answer is simple and straight-forward: Creating a title in Premiere Pro is easy, looks great, and avoids switching out to a different program. (In fact, you have more text styling controls in Titler than you do in Photoshop!)

Most of the time, we want to key (superimpose) text on video. Premiere's Titler has similar styling controls to Photoshop, but available inside Premiere. If you want to animate a title, After Effects is the best choice. But, a lot of the time, we just want to create a nice title, have it fade in, hold for a while, then fade out.

After Effects is overkill for this. Photoshop requires extra steps. Instead, create your titles directly in Premiere.

To create a new title do *one* of the following:

- Type **Command+T** (**Control+T** on Windows).

- Choose **File > New > Title**.

(Continued)

- Choose **Title** > **New Title** and then choose a title type.

- In the Project panel, press the **New Item** button and choose **Title**.

Specify a name for the title and click **OK**. (In this example, I used the somewhat generic "New Title." Image size and aspect ratio in this dialog will match the sequence settings. The new title is automatically saved when you exit the Titler window, or save the Project file.

Note: Titles are added to the Project panel automatically and are saved as part of the project file.

A Fast Way to Scale and Position Text

Resizing your text is drag-and-drop easy

Here's a fast way to change the size of text in the Titler: grab a corner of the bounding box surrounding the text and drag!

- Hold the **Shift** key while dragging the bounding box to scale the text inside it proportionately.

- Hold the **Option** key while dragging to scale from the center.

- Drag near, but not on, a corner dot to rotate the text.

- Drag inside the bounding box to reposition the text in the frame.

Create a Title based on the Current Title

Here's a fast way to duplicate your creative wizardry

You've created this great new title—designed, styled, and placed it to perfection. Now, you want to use it as the source of another title. Easy.

- In the Titler, open or select the title on which you want to base a new title.

(Continued)

- In the set of controls in the top center of the Titler window, click the **New Title Based On Current Title** icon. (You could also select **Title > New Title > Based on Current Title**, but it takes longer.)

- In the New Title dialog box, enter a name for the new title and click **OK**.

Add new text as needed and close the Titler window.

Open a Title for Editing

This is a simple thing, but if you don't know, it will drive you nuts

Double-click the title in the Project panel or in a Timeline panel.

Note: Titles open in the Titler window, not the Source Monitor.

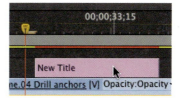

Export, or Import, a Title as an Independent File

It's easy to share titles between projects, or editors

Sharing titles between projects and editors is easy using export and import. When you export a title, Premiere creates a stand-alone file with a .prtl extension. This file can be sent anywhere fine titles need to be sent.

To export a title:

- Select the title you want to save in the Project panel.

- Choose **File > Export > Title**.

- Specify a name and location for the file and click **Save**.

(Continued)

223

To import a title:

- Choose **File > Import**.

- Select a title and click **Open**. The title is imported into the Project panel.

Note: If you share titles between computers, make sure that each system includes all the fonts, textures, logos, and images used in the original title.

Show Video Behind The Title

This makes it easy to align titles for complex images

By default, the Titler shows the video under the playhead in the Timeline panel. You can toggle this on or off using the **Show Video** button in the top center portion of the Titler toolbar. (This video display frame is for your reference only; it is not saved as part of the title.)

You can change the frame displayed in the Titler window by dragging the yellow timecode numbers immediately below this button left or right. (If the numbers are gray, click the **Show Video** button to display the video and enable the timecode slider.)

Note: You can also change the frame displayed in the Titler by moving the playhead in the Timeline.

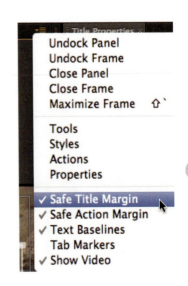

Display Safe Margins in the Titler

Safe margins are also called action safe and title safe

By default, Safe Margins are turned on in the Titler. In the event they are not, turn them on, or off, by clicking the fly-out menu just to the left of the Title Properties tab.

224

(Continued)

- **Safe Title Margin** displays a rectangle 10 percent in from all edges. Keep all essential text and logos inside this area.

- **Safe Action Margin** displays a rectangle 5 percent in from all edges. Keep all essential action and actors inside this somewhat larger area.

Safe Margins Still Matter

Pay attention to action safe and title safe, even for the web

Programs created for broadcast or cable need to pay attention to Action Safe and Title Safe, what Adobe groups into Safe Margins.

However, even if you are creating programs for the web or DVD, these framing areas can help. That's because when you position elements on the screen (like text and logos), video is not often seen edge to edge. If you're publishing to a television set, DVD, or Blu-ray Disc, you'll often lose part of the picture.

For broadcast and cable programs, all text elements should be kept inside the inner rectangle (called *Title Safe*, which is 10 percent in from all edges). All elements that are meant to be seen, like actors, should be kept inside the outer rectangle (called *Action Safe*, which is 5 percent in from all edges). These percentages can be adjusted in **Project > Project Settings > General**.

For web videos or digital projection, I recommend keeping all essential elements—graphics, text, logos, and actors - inside the *Safe Action Margin* rectangle.

An earlier tip explained how to display Safe Margins in the Titler. To display them in either the Source or Program monitors, click the wrench icon in the lower right corner of the Source or Program monitors and select **Safe Margins**.

Note: Action Safe and Title Safe are often described as covering 10 percent of the screen and 20 percent of the screen. For example, Title Safe is 10 percent in from each edge, which means it represents 20% (10% + 10%) horizontally and 20 percent vertically.

225

Access Templates for your Titles

Templates save time and provide a starting point for customization

Adobe ships over a gigabyte of additional content for Premiere Pro and Encore. This includes title templates, as well as a wide variety of other goodies. Adobe calls it: "Adobe Premiere Pro CS6 Functional Content."

To see if you have downloaded this material, go to **Title > Templates**. If the Title Designer Presets is empty, click the words "Title Designer Presets" to display a link to download this material.

Once downloaded, install these files like any other application.

Select a Title Template

Templates make reusing work fast and simple

Adobe has created a *vast*, well, OK, a really, really large, collection of templates that you can use for your titles.

They are grouped by category, with a small preview window so you can see what they look like. Some templates, like the one in this screen shot, have transparent backgrounds, represented by dark and light gray squares which allow you to key the title over an existing clip.

(Continued)

- To display templates, select **Title > Templates** (type **Command+J** (or **Control+J** for Windows).

- To change a template, simply select a different template. However, this also resets any text you've already entered back to the default text for that template.

- You can modify a template, then save it as a title to use in your project, or save it as a template (more on that in a tip or two).

Load a Template for a New Title

Here's a fast way to create a new title from a template

If you know you want to use an existing template to create a new title, save time and choose the template directly:

- Choose **Title > New Title > Based On Template**.

- Click the triangle next to a category name to expand it.

- Select the template, and then click **OK**.

Create a Template from an Open Title

I love this trick—easily save an existing title to reuse as a template

After creating a title, it's easy to reuse it by simply saving it as a separate file. But, if this is a title design I plan to reuse it a lot, it's better to save this as a template. Unlike separate files, which could be stored anywhere and need to be tracked down, titles saved as templates show up in the User Templates category in the Templates window.

(Continued)

- With a title open, click the **Templates** icon, type **Command+J**, (**Control+J**) or select **Title > Templates**.

- From the fly-out menu in the top right corner, choose **Import Current Title As Template**.

- Enter a name for the title template, and then click **OK**.

This takes the currently open title and saves it as a template and stores it in the User Templates category.

Now, whenever you need to reuse it, simply select it from the User Templates category in the Templates window.

Import a Saved Title File as a Template

Here's a fast way to use an existing title as a template

If you have an existing title saved as a separate file that you want to use as a template for a new title:

- Create a new title, or open an existing one.

- Choose **Title > Templates**.

- Click the small, right-pointing arrow in the top right corner.

- Choose **Import File As Template**.

- Select a file, and click **Choose** (Mac OS) or **Open** (Windows). You can only import Premiere Pro title files (.prtl) as templates.

- Give the template a name and then click **OK**.

Your existing title file will not be changed in this process.

Set or Restore a Default Template

Setting a default template can speed the creation of multiple titles

Just as default transitions speed the process of adding transitions, a default title template simplifies the process of creating, say, similar lower-third titles. By using the template, you only need to add new text; all the design work is complete.

- With a title open, click the **Templates** icon (or type **Command+J**–**Control+J** for Windows) and select a template.

- From the small fly-out menu in the top right corner of the Templates panel, choose **Set Template As Default Still**. This default template loads each time you create a new title and open the Titler.

- To restore the default set of templates, choose **Restore Default Templates** from the Templates panel menu.

- Click **OK**.

This same menu also allows you to restore the default set of templates, rename a template, or delete a template. Only user-created templates can be renamed or deleted.

Note: If you delete a template using this procedure, it is removed from the hard disk.

How to Create a Still Frame

Creating still frames can be done, but it's awkward

Still frames, or freeze frames, or hold frames (the terms are used interchangeably) allow you to freeze the action in a clip. While Premiere allows

(Continued)

you to freeze the beginning or the end of a clip, **Clip > Frame Hold**, most of the time, we want to freeze the action in the middle of the clip.

To do this:

- Put the playhead on the frame you want to freeze in either the Source or Program monitors.

- Click the **Export to Still Frame** button in the play controls at the bottom of the appropriate monitor.

- Import the exported still into Premiere and edit it into the Timeline.

Weird and awkward, but it works.

Note: A quick workaround for this is to cut a clip where you want to add a freeze-frame and use **Clip > Frame Hold** to freeze the frame at the cut.

How to Change the Speed of a Clip

Premiere CS6 makes changing clip speed simple

To change the speed of a clip by the same amount, select the clip and choose **Clip > Speed/Duration**.

You can also use this dialog to reverse a clip (play it from back to front), and change clip speed by entering the duration you want the clip to fill.

Note: By default, Premiere does not change the duration of the clip when you change the speed. This means that the Out of the original clip is ignored, with either fewer source frames played (when the clip is slowed down) or more source frames played (when the clip is sped up.) To change this behavior, check the **Ripple Edit, Shifting Trailing Clips** checkbox. This plays every frame from the In to the Out of the clip, regardless of speed, but it always changes the duration of the clip in the Timeline.

How to Vary the Speed of a Clip During Playback

Time remapping allows clip speed to vary during playback

To vary the speed of a clip during playback, select the clip, then go to the Effect Controls panel and twirl down **Time Remapping**.

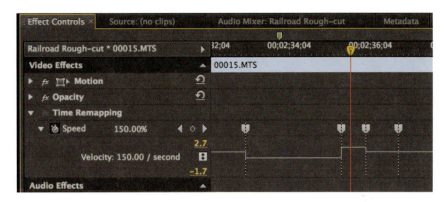

- Position the playhead in the Effect Controls panel where you want a speed change to occur.

- Set a speed keyframe by either clicking the stop watch icon for the first keyframe, or the open diamond for succeeding keyframes.

- Drag the white horizontal line to the right of the keyframe up or down to set the clip speed for that section.

- If you want multiple speed changes in the same clip, add a keyframe for each speed change.

Put the playhead above the line you are changing to view the percentage of change. (You can't simply enter a speed value here, you need to drag the white lines.)

To reset a clip back to its default 100 percent speed, click the stopwatch icon to the left of the word: "Speed." This removes all speed keyframes from the clip.

How to Create Slow Motion From Faster Frame Rate Clips

Use interpret footage to reset clip speed

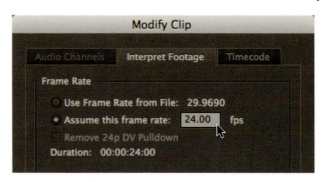

A common way to create a slow-motion (slomo) effect is to shoot at a faster frame rate in the camera, then play that clip back at a slower frame rate in the Timeline. (NFL Films is legendary for using this technique.)

Unfortunately, Premiere always wants to play a clip at the speed it was recorded. But there is a simple fix. Let's say your Timeline is set for 24 fps (23.976, actually), but you shot your video at 60 fps (or any speed faster than 24).

- Select the clip you want to slow down in the Project panel.

- Right-click the clip and select **Modify > Interpret Footage**.

- In the Frame Rate section, click the second radio button and set the frame rate to whatever rate you want.

Ta-DAH! Instant slow motion, without any rendering.

A Fast Way to Resize an Image in the Program Monitor

Size and rotate an image in one easy move

You want to build a picture-in-picture effect—for instance, in this case, we want to illustrate how to build model railroad scenery.

Stack two, or more, clips in the Timeline, with the foreground clip on the higher track. Then, in the Program Monitor, double-click the image. (I use the word

(Continued)

image to refer to the video portion of a clip. This image can be moving or still.)

A white bounding-box appears around the image.

- Drag any dot to scale the image from the center.

- Hold the **Option** key while dragging to scale a wireframe, which is faster than scaling a large image.

- Drag outside the image, but near a dot to rotate (watch for the cursor to change shape)

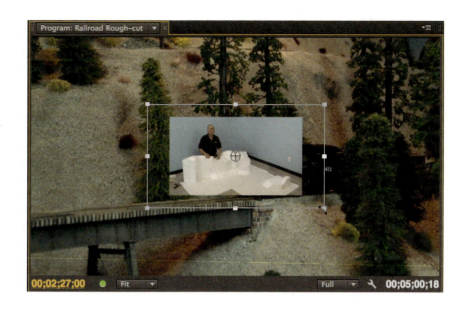

A Fast Way to Reposition an Image in the Program Monitor

Dragging is the key

Once you select an image in the Program Monitor by double-clicking, you can also reposition it anywhere in or out of the frame by clicking inside the image and dragging.

If you can't see the bounding box for the image, click the **Fit** pop-up menu in the lower left side of the monitor (just to the right of the timecode numbers) and reduce the scale of the image. This just changes the image display in the monitor and does not affect the size of your image in the Timeline.

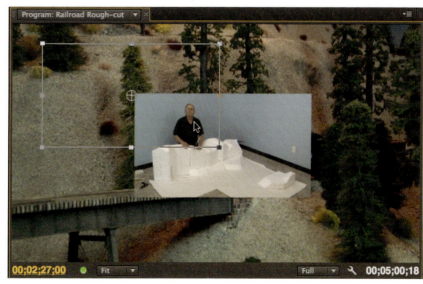

(Continued)

If an image extends outside the frame, you only see the portion of the image inside the frame.

Note: Hold the **Option** key while dragging allows you to drag a wireframe. When you let go of the mouse, the image fills the wireframe. This is a hold-over from when computers were much slower, but it is still a fast way to reposition very large images, or images using complex codecs.

Reset an Image to its Default Settings

Just in case you make a mistake …

If you ever want to reset a clip back to its default settings, you need to use the Reset button. But, um, where is it?

You can't reset everything back to default with one click. In most cases, you wouldn't want to. However, you *can* reset individual filters, audio effects, or video effects.

Click a clip to select it—you don't need to double-click it—and go to the Effect Controls panel, located in the same section of the interface as the Source window.

Click the curved arrow next to the parameter you want to reset. For instance, to reset a clip back to 100 percent full screen and remove any scale, rotation, or position settings you may have applied, click the Reset button for Motion. (The screen shot indicates where to click.)

Poof. All well better.

A Faster Way to Apply an Effect

Now, effects are only a double-click away

The fastest way to apply an effect to a selected clip, or selected group of clips, is to open the Effects panel and double-click the effect you want to apply.

For instance, here, I am desaturating (removing the color of) several selected clips by double-clicking **Effects > Video Effects > Image Control > Black & White.**

Done.

A Better Way to Create Effects

Change your workspace to make effects easier to create

One of the benefits of selectable workspaces is that you can change the Premiere interface in a heartbeat. This makes a lot of sense when you need to start creating effects.

Select **Window > Workspace > Effects,** or type **Option+Shift+5 (Alt+Shift+5** for Windows). This displays the Info, Effects, and Effect Controls tabs to make it easier to adjust effects.

The key to using this workspace properly is to put the playhead in the middle of the clip to which you want to add effects, then select the clip, or adjustment layer, you want to adjust. This displays the clip in the Program Monitor, with all the effects settings readily available.

You can adjust effects *and* see the changes in real-time.

(Continued)

Removing Selected Effects

Need to remove only some of the effects attached to a clip? Easy

If you need to remove some of the effects from a clip—say a filter—without removing other effects—say scale and repositioning—it's easy.

- Select the clip.

- Choose **Clip > Remove Effects**.

- Check the effects you want to remove and click **OK**.

Done.

Discovering Work Areas

Work areas create a faster way to render

A work area is not the same as a workspace. A work area is a range within a sequence that simplifies rendering. Specifically, rather than render an entire sequence, you can render just the work area.

The work area is illustrated by the light gray bar at the top of the Timeline and, by default, spans the entire duration of a sequence. However the work area can be as short as a transition, or as long as your entire sequence.

Double-click the gray work area bar and it expands to either fill the Timeline panel, or cover your entire sequence, whichever is shorter.

Create an In by either dragging the orange indicator on the left, or type **Option+[** (**Alt+[** on Windows). Change the Out by either dragging the orange indicator on the right, or type **Option+]** (**Alt+]** on Windows).

Reposition the work area in the Timeline by dragging it in the middle.

Press the **Return** key to render all effects located in the work area.

237

A Better Way to Apply Effects

Premiere pro CS6 inherits adjustment layers from after effects, which got 'em from photoshop

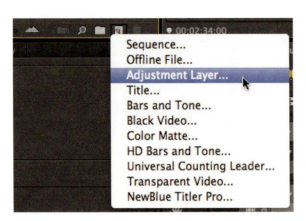

Adjustment layers are a big new feature in CS6. Adjustment layers, as we learned in Photoshop, allow us to create effects which apply to a portion of a clip, an entire clip, a range of clips, or all clips on all layers *below* the adjustment layer. (But not tracks above it—this allows us to create effects which apply to the background, for example, without affecting the foreground.)

Another benefit of adjustment layers is that we can create an effect which applies to multiple clips but only needs to be adjusted in one place. Also, adjustment layers are easy to remove, without having to remove effects on a clip-by-clip basis.

The easiest way to create an Adjustment Layer is to click the **New Item** icon in the lower right corner of the Project panel.

Note: If you've zoomed the whole Premiere Pro interface to a small size, or you are running the program on a small monitor, you can also create an adjustment layer by right-clicking a clip and selecting **Adjustment Layer**.

Once you've created an adjustment layer, place it above the clips you want it to affect, and apply an effect to it. That will affect all layers of video *under* the adjustment layer. You can also resize and reposition the adjustment layer so that the effect only applies to a portion of the image frame.

Note: While you can apply an adjustment layer to a single clip, in most cases it will be easier to apply the effects directly to the clip. Adjustment layers are best used for applying the same effect—and settings—to multiple clips or ranges within a clip.

Adding Effects to an Adjustment Layer

Adjustment layers are just like clips—only a bit different

You apply effects to an adjustment layer as though it were a clip:

- Select the adjustment layer.

- Locate the effect you want to apply to the layer in the Effects panel.

- Double-click the effect to apply it.

You can apply multiple effects to one adjustment layer. Remember that the effect(s) in an Adjustment Layer apply the same settings to all the clips below it.

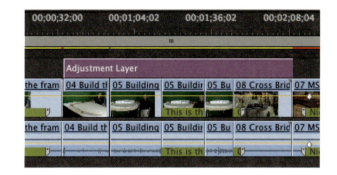

Deleting Effects Contained in an Adjustment Layer

The process is the same as deleting effects applied to a clip

To delete one, or more, effects applied to an Adjustment Layer select the layer, then, in the Effect Controls tab, select the *name* of the effect you want to delete.

Press **Delete** to remove the selected effects.

Note: **Command-click** (**Cntrl-click** on Windows) to select more than one effect. You can only delete effects that you have applied. Motion, Opacity, and Time Remapping effects can't be deleted, only reset.

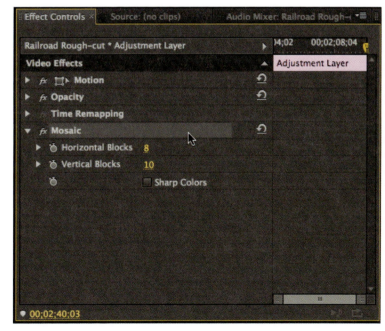

239

Modifying an Adjustment Layer

We can modify its location, duration, name—just like a clip

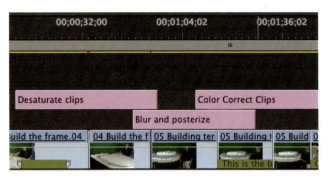

Adjustment layers can be modified similar to clips:

- Drag the In to adjust the starting position of the effect.

- Drag the Out to adjust the ending position of the effect.

- Slide the middle of the layer to adjust its position in the Timeline.

You can also stack adjustment layers to apply different effects to different ranges of clips.

To delete an adjustment layer, and all the effects it contains, select it, and press the **Delete** key.

Note: You can also rename adjustment layers—to help you remember what effects are in that layer—right-click on an adjustment layer and select **Rename**.

Explaining Dynamic Linking

This provides the ability to send files and projects between apps without rendering

Dynamic linking saw major improvements in the CS6 release. It is faster, more stable, and works between the applications that are part of Production Premium and the same applications if purchased separately.

You can dynamically link between Premiere Pro, After Effects, Audition, and Encore. This allows you to quickly send a file from Premiere to After Effects, make changes to it, then send it back—all without rendering. (It's the "without rendering" phrase that makes this process so attractive.)

240

(Continued)

However, complex After Effects may take a while to render inside Premiere. If you run into this problem, here are three things you can to reduce playback delays:

- Take the linked composition off-line.

- Disable a linked clip to temporarily stop referencing a composition.

- Render the composition in After Effects and replace the dynamically-linked clip in Premiere with the rendered file.

Remember to enable or reconnect a clip before final output of your project.

Dynamically Link Files to Send to After Effects

A one-step method to send clips to after effects

To send a clip, or group of clips, from Premiere to After Effects:

- Select the clip(s) you want to include in the composition.

- Right-click any of the selected clips.

- Select **Replace with After Effects Composition**.

Premiere bundles those clips and sends them to AE, while replacing the clips in the Premiere Timeline with the AE comp.

Create your effect, or make your changes in After Effects, then simply save the composition to have it automatically updated in Premiere.

Edit Original
Edit in Adobe Photoshop
Replace With After Effects Composition
Properties

Link to an Existing After Effects Comp

Easily connect to existing AE projects

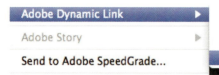

Dynamic linking allows you to make changes to files in other applications without rendering. In fact, you can even link to existing AE projects. Here's how:

- In Premiere, choose **File > Adobe Dynamic Link > Import After Effects Composition**.

- Choose an AE project file and click **Open**.

- Choose one or more compositions from within that AE project and click **OK**.

You can also drag comps from the AE project panel to the Premiere project panel.

At this point, these comps act like clips in Premiere, which you can edit, trim, and manipulate like any other clip.

A Fast Way to Fix Color

This can fix color problems in the blink of an eye(Dropper)

Entire books are written on the subject of color correction. However, you know the drill, the project that has the shortest deadline also has the worst color. You need to fix it—FAST—but don't have the time, or budget, for a complete color grade. Here's a shortcut using the Fast Color Corrector effect that can bail you out.

(Continued)

1. Select the clip you want to color correct.

2. In the Effects panel, apply **Color Correction > Fast Color Corrector**.

3. Double-click the clip to load it into the Source panel and click the Effect Controls tab.

4. Click the eyedropper next to **White Balance** to manually assign a white balance to an image.

5. In the Program monitor, select a color that should be neutral gray. The eyedropper will automatically assign the correct color on the Hue Balance and Angle wheel. If needed, you can further drag inside the wheel to remove additional color casts.

6. If the white balance is still not ideal, drag the **Balance Magnitude** slider. This increases the amount of color balance correction as determined by the Balance Angle.

7. Adjusting **Saturation** modifies the image's color saturation. The default value is **100**, which doesn't affect the colors. Values less than 100 decrease saturation, with 0 completely removing any color. Values greater than 100 produce more saturated colors.

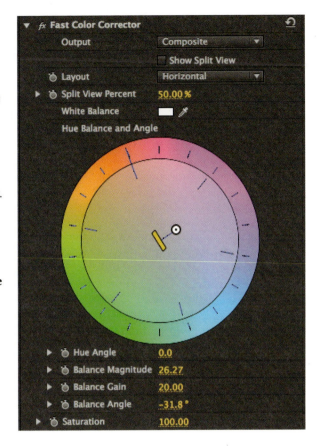

The color controls inside Premiere, and far more with Speed Grade, provide a lot more precision and control. But, when it comes to fast fixes, this filter is a great place to start.

To reset the filter, click the small, hooked arrow at the top right of the filter, next to the words Fast Color Corrector.

Note: When deciding what to use as a color reference in your clip, mid-tone gray is the best choice, followed by lighter gray, then darker gray. Avoid selecting pure white, pure black, speculars, or over-exposed video.

Using the Warp Stabilizer

This image stabilizer moved from after effects to premiere

When it comes time to stabilize hand-held footage, the Warp Stabilizer is the tool to use.

● Select the clip you want to stabilize.

● In the Effects panel, double-click **Distort > Warp Stabilizer** to apply it to the selected clip. (You could also drag the effect on top of the clip, but dragging is much less sexy.)

As soon as the effect is applied, Premiere analyzes the clip in the background. This can take a while (five to ten times the duration of the clip). So feel free to work on other parts of your project while this analysis is going on.

You only need to analyze a clip once, unless you change the In or Out points for a clip, at which point Premiere will re-analyze the clip.

Note: Although the default Stabilization Method is "Subspace Warp," I tend to change this to "Position" first, which generates less artifacts. Feel free to play with different settings to see what looks the best.

Adjust the Smoothness percentage to increase or decrease the stabilization. The shakier the clip, or the greater the amount of stabilization, the more likely you are to have artifacts—weirdness—in the image. There is no magic number, play with different settings until you get the stability you need. Keep in mind that if you want a totally stable image, nothing beats a tripod.

Note: The Premiere Pro help files are a little skimpy on explaining the finer details of this filter. For a more complete description of this filter, look it up in the Adobe After Effects help.

As We Roll Merrily Along

A fast way to correct rolling shutter problems

Another new feature in CS6 is the Rolling Shutter Repair plug-in. One of the problems with many DSLR cameras is that when it takes a photo, there is a short time lag between exposing the top of the image through to exposing the bottom of the image. This lag is not normally a problem unless you are rapidly panning or tilting the camera. At which point, images start to lean ... a lot.

Located in the Effects panel, look for **Distort > Rolling Shutter Repair**, this plug-in corrects this distortion, as well as smear, skew, and wobble.

Note: Although the Warp Stabilizer effect also offers rolling shutter repair, this stand-alone effect has more controls. It also allows you to remove rolling shutter artifacts without also stabilizing the shot.

Finding Blend Modes

You have more control over blend modes than you think

There is a universal blend mode available at the top of the Effect Controls tab in the Opacity section. These give you access to just about everything.

Blend modes allow you to combine textures between two clips based upon either the gray scale or color values in an image. Blend modes always require at least two clips to be stacked on top of each other. Select the top clip when you want to apply a blend mode.

(Continued)

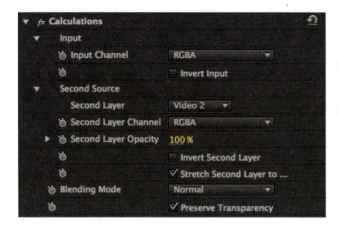

However, there's more you can do with blend modes, if you know where to look.

- Select the top clip then, in the Effects panel select **Channel > Calculations**.

- In the Effect Control tab, twirl down **Calculations** to access the additional Blending Mode controls.

There is so much we can do with effects in Premiere that this chapter simply explained how things work. Describing how to create specific looks, well, that would require a whole separate book.

CHAPTER 10

Premiere Pro Export and Adobe Media Encoder

This is the final step—getting our completed projects out of Premiere and ready to post to the web. And, based solely on my e-mail in-box, export and compression are two subjects that confuse a whole lot of folks. So, let's see if we can clear things up by the end of this chapter.

Change the Media Cache Location

In the CS6 release, Premiere Pro, After Effects, Encore, and Adobe Media Encoder all share the same database (called the *Media Cache Database*).

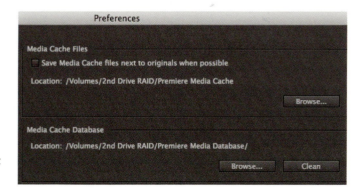

This cache improves performance for previews because they can be rendered once, then accessed multiple times from different applications. It is generally a good idea to make sure this cache is stored on a fast hard disk, generally not your boot drive. (In this example, I've stored it onto an attached RAID.)

(Continued)

Note: However, recent advances in SSD drives make them an attractive alternative for storing cache files.

You can change the cache location by going to **[Name of Application] > Preferences > Media**; Windows users go to: **Edit > Preferences > Media**.

In this preferences dialog, you can also empty the cache, which removes all cache content for which the source media can not by found, by clicking the **Clean** button. Generally, you only need to do this to save space at the end of a project, or if you are running into slow-downs during a project.

Output a Project

Premiere provides lots of options on export

The export window in Premiere, illustrated on the next page, has been known to scare small children. However, before you panic, let's take it in steps.

The left side allows you to select which portion of the project you want to export. It defaults to exporting the work area, or the range between the In and the Out if the work area bar is hidden. However, here you can set a custom In or Out, along with selecting a range from the **Source Range** popup menu under the image.

In general, the highest quality output matches the video you edited. So I tend to check the **Match Sequence Settings** checkbox at the top right of this window.

My recommendation is to export a master file of your project, matching sequence settings, then use that as the source file for all subsequent compression.

Note: However, because Premiere Pro edits camera source images in many cases, not all these formats can be encoded by Premiere on export. For instance, XDCAM content will be encoded to MPEG-2 if you choose "Match Settings." In which case, consider using AVC-Intra (see the next tip).

(*Continued*)

When Exporting to a Higher-Quality Video Format Makes Sense

There are some advantages to exporting to a different format than you edited

Normally, the best option for outputting a project is to export the same format you edited. This is because outputting to a higher quality format—say AVC-Intra—won't improve original image quality. Basically, when it comes to image resolution, focus, interlacing ... what you shoot is what you get.

(Continued)

251

Note: Mac users should consider using ProRes 422, or ProRes 422 HQ. The big benefit to AVC-Intra, which is also an excellent codec, is that it is cross-platform. Mac users that need the ProRes codec can get it free with the purchase of Apple's Compressor application.

However, exporting at higher quality may improve effects render speed and quality, especially with color correction and complex After Effects comps.

How do you decide? If you spent the time on great lighting, crisp focus, color graded each scene on a calibrated monitor, and don't have excessive video noise in your image, you will probably see a difference in quality.

However, if you went with available light, using a handheld camera, with the aperture wide open and lens zoomed wide, you won't see a difference, regardless of how good your color grading is.

Note: Another high-quality codec worth considering for both Mac and Windows is the Cineform codec, which is free on the GoPro website (cineform.com).

Send Image to Photoshop

Premiere can easily share photoshop files

Moving image files between Premiere to Photoshop is easy ... sort of. Let's say you have a JPEG image. Right-click it in the Project panel and, at the bottom, select **Edit in Adobe Photoshop**.

The image opens immediately into Photoshop where you can make whatever changes you need.

Now, you have a choice. If you save the revised file using the exact same file name and extension, Photoshop will replace the existing version with the new version and Premiere automatically updates to the new version of the file.

(Continued)

If, on the other hand, you save it with either a different file name or extension (and Photoshop defaults to saving files with a .PSD extension) then you will need to import the new file into Premiere.

I prefer to save a copy, then relink to the copy inside Premiere. That way, I always have the original source image in case I need it.

Send Sequence to Encore

This is a really fast technique to move projects to DVD or blu-ray

You know the normal drill:

- Export the project
- Compress the project for DVD
- Import the project into Encore

Sigh. Boring, and it takes time.

Premiere makes exporting files to Encore a whole lot easier, because you no longer need to compress them before importing them into Encore. Instead, Premiere passes the compression duties to Encore. Encore then loads these source files and compresses them either when told to do so, or when the disc is burned.

This allows you to get back to editing without wasting time. You can send either complete sequences or portions of sequences. This technique requires that both Premiere Pro and Encore are installed on the same system:

- Select a sequence in the Project panel
- Select **File > Adobe Dynamic Link > Send to Encore**
- Give the DVD project a name and location.

(Continued)

- In Project Settings, select the authoring mode you want to use.

- If you want, click the **Advanced** tab and set any relevant transcoding settings.

- Click **OK**.

At which point, you can fire up Encore and finish authoring your project.

Send Clips to After Effects

A one-step method to send files to after effects

To send a clip, or group of clips, from Premiere to After Effects:

- Select the clip(s) you want to include in the composition

- Right-click any of the selected clips

- Select **Replace with After Effects Composition**

Premiere bundles those clips and sends them to AE, while replacing the clips in the Premiere Timeline with the AE comp. Create your effect, or make your changes in After Effects, then simply save the composition to have it automatically updated in Premiere.

Export to FCP 7

Adobe significantly improved compatibility with final cut studio (3)

It may seem strange for Premiere Pro to export files for Final Cut Pro 7, but a key feature that Adobe focused on in this release was compatibility with a variety of programs in Final Cut Studio (3).

- Prelude exports rough cuts to Premiere or Final Cut.

- Premiere can import or export FCP 7 project files using XML.

254

(Continued)

- Audition accepts projects from Final Cut Pro and Avid Media Composer.

- Adobe Media Encoder compresses media files from just about anything.

- Encore works with media files created in a variety of applications.

What this means to editors is that you are not stuck working in a single application. Adobe easily allows moving files anywhere.

To export a Premiere sequence to Final Cut Pro 7, select the sequence in the Project panel, then choose **File > Export > Final Cut Pro XML**. Give the file a name and location and click **Save**.

How Do You Move A Project To A Different Computer?

Hint: you need to collect your thoughts …

You use Project Manager to consolidate all your project files in one place. The easiest way to move a large project from one computer to another is to:

- Select **Project > Project Manager**

- Click **Collect Files and Copy to New Location**.

- Click the **Browse** button and indicate where you want the files stored.

- Click **OK**.

If you want to copy ALL project files be sure to uncheck **Exclude Unused Clips**.

Note: No dynamic-linked content is recognized by the Project Manager. You will need to gather these files manually after the Project Manager is done.

Export Still Frames Fast

Exporting screen grabs is one-button—or shortcut—easy

Exporting a still image from a video clip is as easy as clicking a single button—or typing a shortcut. Called a frame grab, this process enables you to write a digital image to your disk at the same resolution as the source video.

- Select either the Source Monitor, Program Monitor or Timeline.

- Position the playhead on the frame you want to export, in a clip or sequence.

- Click the **Export Frame** button or type **Shift+E**. (**Control+Shift+E** on Windows).

- The Export Frame dialog box opens. Give the clip a unique name.

- Choose a format from the pop-up menu. You can create DPX, JPEG, PNG, Targa, or TIFF files on a Mac or PC as well as BMP files on a PC. I recommend using TIFF or PNG for the best image quality.

- Give the still image a name, pick a location and click **Choose**.

Note: This technique is also useful when you want to create a still frame to use in an edit.

Find a Missing Export Frame Button

You can't export if you can't find the stupid button

Having a simple button to click to export a frame is great—but what if you can't find the button?

(Continued)

Well, it could be missing for two reasons:

- The main Premiere window is too narrow. Drag it wider and the button will appear.

- The button isn't with the navigation controls.

If the Export Frame button is missing in your layout, you can easily add it from the Button Editor. Click the **Plus** button in the lower right of either the Source or Program monitor to display the Button Editor.

Then, drag the Export Frame button—or any other button you want—from the Editor to the playback controls bar.

What is Interlacing?

Interlacing interweaves two partial images to create a whole image

Interlacing is the bane of my life. All NTSC video (except 24 fps) and PAL video is interlaced. This was a technique invented back in the '30s to solve a number of technical issues regarding image display and transmission.

(Continued)

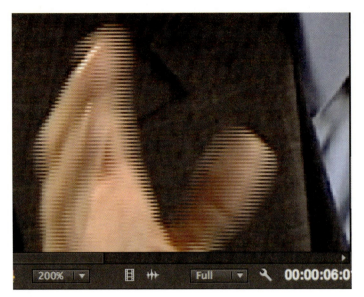

An interlaced image divides the image into alternating horizontal lines. Then, it displays all the odd-numbered lines (Field 1), then, a fraction of a second later, displays all the even-numbered lines (Field 2). The problem is that because these two "fields" are recorded a fraction of a second apart, interlacing creates thin horizontal lines radiating off all moving objects in the frame, as the screen shot illustrates.

This isn't a problem when watching video on a TV screen. However, when we start viewing interlaced video on a computer screen, it looks awful. Interlaced formats include most NTSC and PAL video, as well as the 1080i HD format (the letter "i" means "interlaced."

Premiere hides these interlaced artifacts by default. To show them, click the Wrench icon in the lower right side of either the Source or Program monitors and select **Display Both Fields**.

Need to Deinterlace an Exported Still Frame?

Use photoshop for deinterlacing video screen grabs

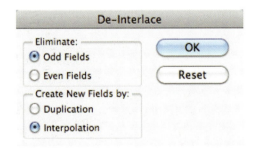

Since interlacing is built into the video image itself, when you export a video still image, the interlacing travels with it. The best way to deinterlace an exported screen grab is using Photoshop.

Once you export your still frame, which we covered in an earlier tip, open it in Photoshop.

Select **Filters > Video > Deinterlace**.

In almost all cases the default settings of this filter will be fine. The only exception is when you are editing video which was recorded from the output

(Continued)

of a video switcher, you may have one image on the odd field and a different image on the even field. Select the appropriate radio button to display the image you want.

Click **OK** and you're done.

Note: By definition, deinterlacing removes vertical resolution from your image; which means a deinterlaced image will be softer than the same image taken progressively. Ideally, shoot progressive video. If that isn't possible, hire a still photographer to take high-res stills during production.

Adobe Media Encoder's New Interface

The AME interface is now more like premiere

The Adobe Media Encoder has a new interface with the CS6 version, which helps it look and act much more like Premiere.

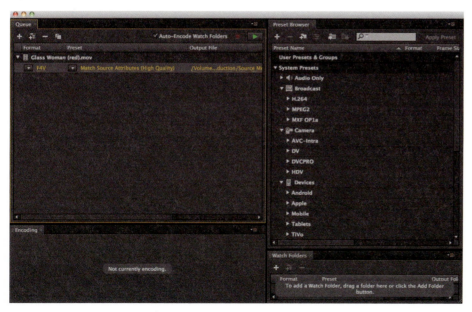

(Continued)

259

Adobe added a new panel—Preset Browser, in the top right quadrant—to the three original panels of Queue, Encoding Status, and Watch Folders. These four panels can be grouped, positioned, sized, docked, floated, and reorganized into a variety of custom combinations.

As we learned with other Adobe applications, you can save any modified layout as a new Workspace so you can reuse it whenever you want. (Though, truthfully, with only four panels, this isn't really necessary.)

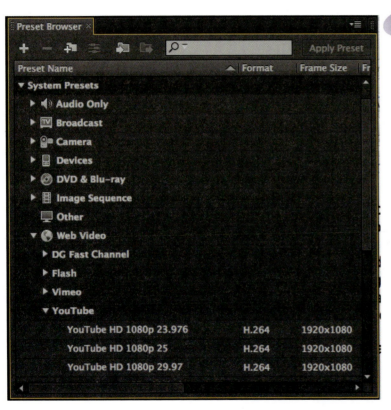

Selecting the Best Preset for the Job

New preset browser organizes compression settings into categories

The Preset Browser groups compression settings—called "Presets"—into categories—called "Preset Groups"—to make it easier to find the right preset for a particular compression task.

For instance, the Web Video category contains presets for Flash, Vimeo, and YouTube.

When selecting a preset it is important to choose a preset based upon the compressed, final version of the file that you want to create. The original format of the media is irrelevant. AME handles all the conversion details, you just need to tell it the final results that you want. The file format and size, of the source file is not important.

Personally, when compressing files for the web, I create 1280 x 720 progressive images at 30 fps.

A Faster Way to Compress a File

Drag and drop projects to speed compression

With Premiere Pro CS6 or Adobe After Effects CS6, you no longer need to export a sequence before you can compress it.

Open Adobe Media Encoder (AME) and drag the Premiere project file (or AE composition) on top of a compression Preset, or Preset Group, in the Preset Browser. This automatically applies the compression setting and moves the file into the Queue panel for compression.

In fact, if you take the time to set up default presets, you can drop the project file directly into the Queue and the default preset and destination are instantly applied. This can save you a TON of time waiting for projects to export, when you no longer need to.

After you drop the project on a preset, the **Import Premiere Pro Sequence** dialog appears. Select the sequence, or sequences, you want to compress and click **OK**. This allows you to compress some sequences without compressing all of them.

Note: Dropping a project on top of a Preset Group creates multiple compressed versions of the sequences in the project.

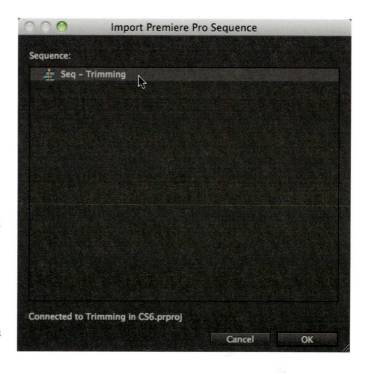

Grouping Presets

Preset groups can contain presets, aliases, or other groups

In Adobe Media Encoder, Adobe organized all the compression presets into categories and subcategories of either how files will be distributed, or what type of screen the final compressed version is intended for.

(Continued)

But, what if you want to organize your images based upon data rate, or screen size, or filter setting? Now, you can. Plus, these new groups can contain a mix of custom and factory presets.

Click the **New Group** icon at the top of the Preset Browser to create a new group (folder).

Note: To put a group inside another group, select the containing group folder before creating the new group.

After you give the new group a name, it appears in the User Presets & Groups section at the top of the Browser.

Drag any existing presets into the new group. Copies of existing presets are indicated by italic text. Or create a custom preset, which is discussed below, and drag it into a folder. There is no limit to the number of presets or folders you can create.

Important Note: You can delete a preset group by selecting it and pressing **Delete**. However, there is no additional warning. The Group is deleted, as are all presets stored within it. Be careful. You can recover from a mistake by using **Undo**.

Store All Your Compressed Files in One Place

Set a custom destination for all compressed files

Something I learned a long time ago is that, unless you pay really close attention, media tends to wander all over your hard disks. Files seem to be stored everywhere. So, I make sure that whenever I compress a file, it always goes to the same place: a custom destination on one of my hard drives.

(Continued)

Here's how:

- On a second drive, I created a folder called: **Compressed Files**.

- Go to **Adobe Media Encoder > Preferences** (Mac) or **Edit > Preferences** (Windows).

- Check **Specify output file destinations.**

- Click the **Browse** button and select the Compressed Files folder.

Now, every time I compress a new file, regardless of where the master file is stored, the compressed version always ends up in the same place.

Set a Default Compression Preset

The more you automate compression, the better it works

Face it, except to a few guys with no social life, compression is boring. Really boring. The less time I spend in Adobe Media Encoder the happier I am. I mean, it's a nice application but, really, is watching video compress the highlight of your day? I didn't think so.

If you are generally compressing the same types of files, set up a custom destination (which we just talked about) and a default compression setting and as fast as you load files, you can get outta there and get some real work done. Here's how:

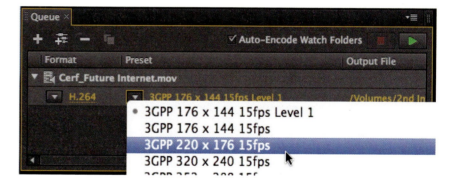

- Import a source file into the Queue.

- Click the downward-pointing arrow in the Preset column and pick the preset you want to use as a default.

(Continued)

Every time you load a new file into the Queue, AME automatically assigns the last preset you used.

Note: For real efficiency, create a Watch Folder, which we cover at the bottom of this page.

Batch Encoding Jobs

One source file can create multiple outputs

In Adobe Media Encoder CS6, you can take a single file and create multiple outputs with it. For example, you need a version for your website, a separate version for YouTube, and a high-data-rate version to serve as a source master for archiving.

Here's how to setup a batch job for a single file:

- Drag or import the source file into the Queue panel.

- Drag and drop presets on your source file in the Queue for all the files you want to create.

- Confirm they are going to the right output location (change the file name, if necessary).

- Click the green **Start Queue** button (or press **RETURN**) to begin compression.

While you first need to create a preset, this method allows you to create custom compression collections. However, most of the time, we want to use the same settings over and over. In this case, using Watch Folders is more efficient.

Create Watch Folders

Watch folders allow complete automation of compression

Watch folders are wonderful. I do almost all my compression using some form of Watch Folders. A Watch Folder is a special kind of folder that AME

(Continued)

"watches." Whenever a file is dropped into that folder—either on a local hard disk or a server—AME grabs it and compresses it into whatever format you specify for files in that folder.

For instance, I create weekly audio podcasts and interviews. I drop the source files into a podcast folder and AME automatically compresses it and transfers it up to my website for publication.

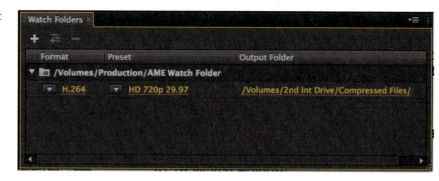

To create a Watch Folder:

- Click the **Plus** button in the top left corner of the Watch Folder panel.

- Navigate to the folder you want AME to watch. It can be local or on a server. (In this case, I created a folder called: **AME Watch Folder**, but you can name the folder anything you want.)

- Select the folder and click **Choose**.

- Assign a **Format**. In the screen shot, I selected H.264.

- Assign a **Preset**. I selected HD 720p 29.97.

- Assign an **Output Volume**. Think of this as the output file path. For example, this was the Compressed Files folder we discussed earlier.

Make sure the checkbox **Auto-Encode Watch Folders** is checked at the top of the Queue, then click the **Start Queue** button (green arrow) to enable AME to scout for files in the Watch Folder.

At this point, anytime I drop a file into the AME Watch Folder, it will be compressed to these specs and stored in the Compressed Files folder.

Creating Multiple Outputs from One Watch Folder

When it comes to saving time, this technique is a real winner

I create new video training on a variety of subjects every week. And, every week, I need to create:

- A version to post to my website for download

- A version to post to my website for streaming

- A version to load to YouTube

- A high-res version of the master file for archiving.

This technique makes my life a lot easier.

Follow all the steps to create a Watch Folder, detailed in the earlier tip. Then, to that Watch Folder, assign all the different compression preset settings that you need to create.

Now, when you drop a file into this Watch Folder, AME will create as many different versions of the file as you have assigned presets to the Watch Folder.

Why Isn't the Watch Folder Encoding?

Ah, because you haven't turned it on yet

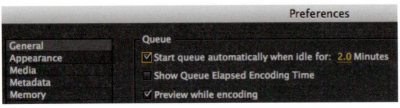

AME only checks Watch Folders when the queue is running. Which means that you need to leave AME running in order for it to check Watch Folders. Also, you need to start the queue before compression will start.

(Continued)

But there's one more essential preference you need to turn on, because it is off by default:

- Go to **Adobe Media Encoder > Preferences** (Mac) or **Edit > Preferences** (Windows).

- The General section is highlighted.

- Check **Start Queue Automatically when idle for 2.0 minutes** (you can set this to any numeric value you want).

What this does is start the queue automatically after the duration you specify, look inside the Watch Folder and, if there's something in it, compress it.

If you don't check this checkbox, you would need to start AME manually and start the queue—which sort of defeats the purpose of having a Watch Folder in the first place.

What Determines the Size of a Compressed File?

Bit rate. Totally and completely

The *size* of a file is based solely on how many bits per second it takes to play the file. Therefore, you could create an impossibly small file by setting the bit rate close to zero.

However, that isn't the right question. Let me explain.

Image quality is based on four criteria:

- **Bit rate**. The higher the bit rate, the better the image quality, but the larger the file size.

- **Image size**. The larger the image, the higher the bit rate needs to be to display it properly.

(Continued)

267

- **Frame rate**. The faster the frame rate, the higher the bit rate needs to be to play all these frames properly.

- **Movement**. The more movement in a scene, the higher the bit rate needs to be to display it properly.

When bit rate is set too low for the image size, frame rate or movement, artifacts, like blocky rectangles, appear randomly in your image.

So compressing a file is a balancing act between getting the bit rate as low as possible to create the smallest file, yet not so low that compression artifacts start to appear.

If it was easy, books would not be written about this subject.

Creating Custom Presets

Every preset can be customized, or you can create your own

Just as books have been written on color correction, books are written on video compression. Let me simply state that we can create an unlimited number of custom compression presets for audio or video.

To create a new, custom preset:

- Click the **Plus** icon in the top left corner of the Preset Browser.

- Complete each of the five tabs of the screen—*Filters, Video, Audio, Multiplexer,* and *FTP*.

- Review your settings in the Summary section near the top.

- When you are happy, click **OK**.

The completed preset is displayed in the User Presets section at the top of the Preset Browser.

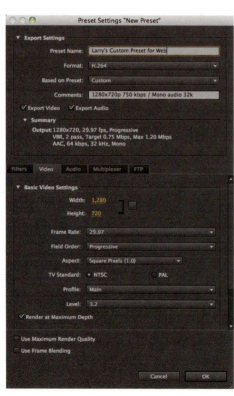

268

(Continued)

Note: It may be easier to start with an existing preset and customize it by adding filters, or modifying settings. Changing a factory preset makes a copy of it and stores it in the User Presets section. You can't change a factory preset without making a copy of it.

Apply Custom Presets to a Watch Folder

Any preset can be applied to a watch folder, including custom settings

Just as we can apply factory presets to a Watch Folder setting, we can also apply custom settings. The only rule is that you need to create the custom preset before creating the Watch Folder.

Well, OK, that's not quite true. You can always change the setting to a Watch Folder. However, you still need to create the setting before you can apply it.

To change a setting for a Watch Folder, click the downward-pointing arrow next to the Preset name next to the folder name in the Watch Folder and select the preset you want to modify.

Review or Modify a Preset Assigned to a Clip

You can modify a preset on a clip-by-clip basis

Once you've applied a preset to a clip, you can review or modify the settings by double-clicking the name of the preset in either the Preset Browser or the Queue, as illustrated on the next page.

Opening the Preset in the Queue allows you to change the settings for that particular clip, without affecting the preset stored in the Preset Browser.

(Continued)

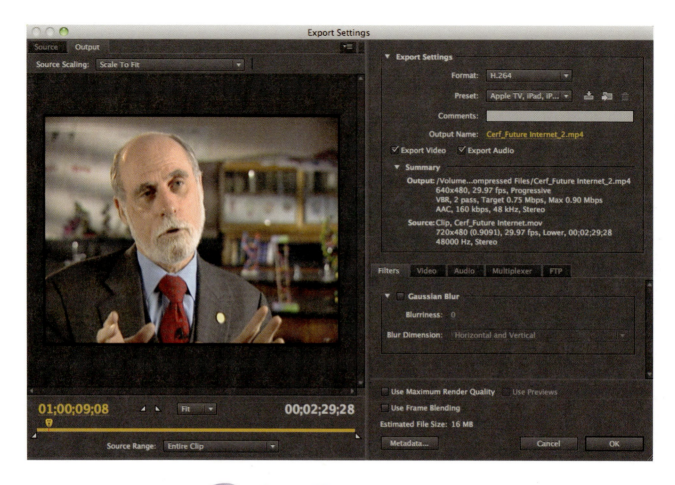

Cropping a Clip

You can crop to create your own image sizes or work within established aspect ratios

Cropping an image allows you to hide something in the frame, reduce the image size, or change the aspect ratio of the finished movie.

(Continued)

You must crop the entire clip by the same amount, you can't keyframe cropping. To crop a clip:

- Double-click a preset in the Queue to open the Export Settings window.

- Click the **Source** tab in the top left corner of the window.

- Click the **Crop** in the top left corner.

- Either enter numeric values for the crop, or draw a rectangle on screen where you want the crop to occur. (In real life, I do both.)

- If you need the crop constrained to an aspect ratio, select the ratio from the pop-up menu with the word **None** on it.

- When you are done making changes to the clip and its compression settings, click **OK**.

Create Transcode Options for Prelude

Improve the quality of your prelude transcodes via custom presets

There are two limitations when using AME for transcoding (which means to convert from one format to another):

- Factory presets are designed for final output and delivery, not transcoding.

- Frame rates cannot be passed through—you need a separate preset for each frame rate you may encounter.

(Continued)

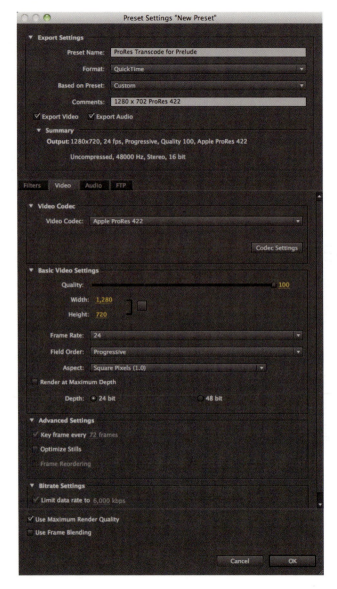

Neither of these are unworkable, but they do create challenges.

For Mac users, ProRes is an excellent transcoding format. For Windows users, consider using AVC-Intra or Cineform. To create a ProRes preset:

- Create a new preset.

- Give it a name—in this case, I used "ProRes Transcode for Prelude".

- Set Format to **QuickTime**.

- Make sure both **Export Video** and **Export Audio** are checked (unchecking one of these means it won't export).

- Click the **Video** tab.

- Mac users should set the Video Codec to **Apple ProRes 422** (or **ProRes 422 HQ**).

- Windows users should set the Video Codec to **AVC-Intra**.

- Set Video Quality to **100%**.

- Set frame size to **1280 x 720** (or **1920 x 1080**, your choice).

- Set frame rate to whatever is appropriate for your clips.

- Field order to **Progressive**.

- Click the **Audio** tab.

- Set Audio Codec to **Uncompressed**.

- Set Sample Rate to **48,000 Hz**.

- Set Channels as appropriate.

(Continued)

- Set Sample Size to **16-bit**.

- Check **Maximum Render Quality**.

- Click **OK**.

This preset will show up in both Prelude and Adobe Media Encoder.

Import/Export Presets

This allows sharing presets between computers

If you need to share presets between systems, start by exporting them.

- Create a preset you like.

- Select it in the Preset Browser.

- Click the **Export Preset** icon in the tool bar at the top.

- Give the file a name and location.

- Click **Save**.

Then, transfer the file to another computer system. To import the file:

- Click the **Import Preset** icon in the tool bar at the top.

- Navigate to the preset file.

- Click **Open**.

The preset shows up on the new system as though it had been created there.

Customize Keyboard Shortcuts

Modifying the existing shortcuts is easy—just as you'd expect

Just as with other Adobe applications, Adobe Media Encoder ships with a wide variety of keyboard shortcuts. (In fact, listing them takes several pages in the Help files.)

However, these, too, can be modified. To modify or create your own keyboard shortcuts:

● Go to **Adobe Media Encoder CS6 > Keyboard Shortcuts**.

● Search for, or navigate to the menu to which you want to assign a shortcut.

● Double-click in the shortcut field you want to modify and enter the shortcut.

● Click **OK** when you are done.

Afterword

We've covered hundreds of tips, shortcuts, and workarounds in this book, and I still feel there are hundreds more to cover.

The process of learning software, and becoming more efficient with it, is never-ending. I study this stuff every day, all day, and even after all these years, I still discover new techniques every week. As you discover new ideas, tips, or hints, let me know. I'll keep track of them and add them to the next revision of this book.

I'm grateful for the time you spent with this book. Just remember, we aren't judged on the tools we use, but on the stories we tell. My goal is to help you tell those stories faster, better, and with less stress by understanding how all these tools work.

I'm looking forward to seeing what you create!

Thanks.

Index

Export Frame button 256–7
Export Preview Video 177
extend edit 140–1
external drives, internal drives vs. 8

Undock Panel 87, 105
USB drives, for video
    editing 5

V

video: configuring tracks 132;
    default transitions 215,
    216; formats 10,
    18-9; importing
    file 182; monitor 94;
    resolution 21-2
video editing 134;
    challenges for 102; hard
    drives for 6-7; USB
    drives for 5
VST 203

W

warp stabilizer effect 244
Watch Folders: automation
    of compression 264-5;
    custom presetting
    to 269; encoding 266-7;
    outputs from 266
Waveform Audio 70
Waveform editor, saving
    files from 212
window, zooming on 75
work areas, discovering 237
workspaces 85, 138;
    customizing 60-1, 88-9;
    reset 62, 89; saving 61-2
wrench icon 90-1, 119-20

X

XML file 185-6

Z

zooming: sequence in
    timeline 112; on
    window 75